'I felt pulled toward my grandmother and an urgent desire to find other parallels between our experiences as musical girls. I wanted to explore how our experiences reflected those of other girls drawn from the pages of history and fiction who had sat at the piano over the course of its history. I came to believe that setting aside Alice's mask of old age might help me to understand my own voyage around the piano—and help me to find my way back.'

'Staring into the piano's black mirror was like seeing into the future, glimpsing the girl I would become, the girl who could play the piano and understand the world around her through her fingertips, and let her hands speak for her when she could not.'

GIRLS at the PIANO

VIRGINIA LLOYD

ALLEN&UNWIN
SYDNEY • MELBOURNE • AUCKLAND • LONDON

First published in 2018

This project has been assisted by the Australian Government through the Australia Council, its arts funding and advisory board.

Allen & Unwin
83 Alexander Street
Crows Nest NSW 2065
Australia
Phone: (61 2) 8425 0100
Email: info@allenandunwin.com
Web: www.allenandunwin.com

A catalogue record for this book is available from the National Library of Australia

ISBN 978 1 76029 777 0

Internal design by Romina Panetta
Set in 12.5/20 pt Bembo Std by Bookhouse, Sydney
Printed and bound in Australia by Griffin Press

10 9 8 7 6 5 4 3 2 1

The paper in this book is FSC® certified. FSC® promotes environmentally responsible, socially beneficial and economically viable management of the world's forests.

for Nate

From this I reach what I might call a philosophy; at any rate it is a constant idea of mine; that behind the cotton wool is hidden a pattern; that we—I mean all human beings—are connected with this; that the whole world is a work of art; that we are parts of the work of art. Hamlet *or a Beethoven quartet is the truth about this vast mass that we call the world. But there is no Shakespeare, there is no Beethoven; certainly and emphatically there is no God; we are the words; we are the music; we are the thing itself.*

Virginia Woolf, 'A Sketch of the Past'

I

'You're going to have two children, a boy and a girl,' the clairvoyant told my mother Pamela, when she was thirty-five and desperate for a baby. In Hunters Hill, a kind of Stepford-upon-Sydney, childlessness was next to godlessness. Especially after a decade of marriage.

It might have been 1968, but there were no outward signs of revolution or even social unrest in the leafy peninsula where the Lane Cove and Parramatta Rivers flow into Sydney Harbour. All that awkward business was in the 1840s, when convicts escaping from nearby Cockatoo Island swam to shore and hid in the densely forested finger of land known as *Moocooboola*, or meeting of waters, to its original inhabitants. Despite the pill and the war in Vietnam, Hunters Hill was the peninsula that time forgot. John hunted and gathered, while Pam cooked and cleaned. When she wasn't doing either of those things, my mother attended meetings of the local chapter of the Young Wives club. One hundred years after the publication of Louisa May Alcott's *Good Wives*, these young married women were the living sequel to *Little Women*. But *young* is a more forgiving adjective for a wife than *good*. In real life, the one mistake a good wife could not make was that she be infertile. In desperation, Pamela followed the recommendation of her hairdresser, whom she consulted more regularly than any priest, and made an appointment with a clairvoyant.

'I don't want you to speak,' the clairvoyant said when she opened the door to her apartment, decked out in a flowing white caftan. 'That's how I do business. I don't want you to give me any information whatsoever.'

She ushered Pamela inside and they sat down across from each other at a square wooden table in an otherwise sparse room. Natural light seeped through drawn curtains.

'You have no children,' the clairvoyant announced, as if it were news to the good wife sitting across from her. 'Don't worry about it, dear, you're going to have two.'

Pamela's eyes widened. She couldn't see how that would happen. None of her doctors had ever spoken with confidence about her chances of conceiving.

'You're going to have the girl first, then the boy three years later,' the clairvoyant continued.

Enchanted by the authority of her prediction, my mother never imagined its every detail would come true. More than forty years later, though she struggles to remember what she did yesterday, my mother recalls the prescient woman's exact words.

'There's one other thing you should know,' she added, with a performer's gift of timing. 'Your daughter is going to be very musical.'

2

Do you still play the piano?

At my twentieth high school reunion, it was the only question anyone had for me. Nobody cared whether I was married or divorced, gay or straight; when I had left my home town of Sydney, or for how long I had lived in New York. The reunion coincided with a trip home, and curiosity about my former classmates got the better of me. I'd had no contact with the vast majority of them since leaving school.

The truth was that I had been widowed more than three years earlier when my husband John died of cancer. I had moved to New York to try to figure out what to do with myself, and I still didn't have a clue. This wasn't the sort of self-portrait you could sketch after a quick *hello* and a *you're looking well*, even if you wanted to. Most people—and especially those at a high school reunion—want executive summaries and concise answers. Unanswerable questions and existential dilemmas are anathema to the high school reunion, which relies on pithy anecdotes, funny stories and bad news of former classmates relayed with a dash of schadenfreude. Stories are everything at the school reunion, except when you've got the wrong kind to tell. Mine wasn't the sort of tale anyone wanted to hear, certainly not over a glass of bubbly and a tour of the school's new science and technology wing. Or perhaps they would love to hear about it, but from someone else—otherwise it would be too much like looking directly at the sun.

I felt pathetic at the preparations I had made to come face to brave face with other faces in their late thirties. I'd carefully applied concealer, which usually lay dormant in the cupboard under the bathroom sink. I'd put on a pair of particularly high heels to optimise the length of my legs, which after all these years I still wished were longer. Why

I cared what these women thought about the length of my legs is beyond me. I'd been worried that I would be more wrinkled than my peers, or the only one without a ring on my wedding finger. And appalled at myself for having those thoughts.

My former classmates and I agreed on the balminess of the October evening, how fabulous we all looked, and how we really were 'old girls' now. The regrettable terminology of alumnae put me in mind of livestock trussed up for display. After twenty years, the dynamic remained unchanged: we were still women dressing up for each other.

'Are you still playing the piano?' came the first question, from a woman gripping the stem of her champagne flute as if for balance. It wasn't even 8 p.m. 'You teach piano, don't you?'

Taken aback, I said, 'Actually, I haven't taught piano in years. I worked in book publishing, then—'

'Oh,' she said, clearly disappointed. 'But you still play, don't you? I'll never forget you playing for school assembly all those years.'

For assembly, twice a week for six years. For the choir. For the madrigals a cappella group. For the solo instrumentalists and the aspiring opera singer. I played for anyone who needed an accompanist, and for whoever asked me. The piano was my first love and, from the age of seven, I spent thirteen years studying the instrument and performing classical music, undertaking annual exams and participating in competitions that to this day remain some of my most vivid experiences of success and humiliation.

The onslaught of unanticipated questions from other 'old girls' told me it would be a long night, and my first glass of champagne soon emptied. But before I could find the bar, I saw Astrid approaching. Astrid, the one old girl who distilled everything I had loathed about attending an all-girls school. Even now she was olive-skinned and radiant, a mature version of her fourteen-year-old self, who would have won a contest for prize bitch out of a competitive field. As a pale freckled girl whose braces glinted in the unforgiving Australian sun, I would gaze at Astrid from the corner of my eye in longing and despair. Her hair wasn't a mousy brown, falling straight like water, but a halo of tousled chocolate curls. Her frequent laugh, natural and wide-mouthed, revealed rows of perfect white teeth. She sat in the back row of our classes, at the desk nearest the window, a commanding position that enabled her to monitor events both outside and inside the classroom. Astrid never hesitated to offer an opinion to the teacher, or to answer a question, and being incorrect seemed not to faze her; she would receive news of a wrong answer with a nonchalant shrug, while if I made one mistake I would stew in hot embarrassment for the remainder of the class. 'Grammar is a piano I play by ear, since I seem to have been out of school the year the rules were mentioned,' Joan Didion wrote in her 1976 essay 'Why I Write'. I must have missed the classes on self-esteem. All I knew was that Astrid seemed to understand something about living in the world that I did not. Even now I longed to ask her what it was.

Watching her move in my direction, a huge smile on her face, I became convinced she beamed in the direction of someone just behind me. We had barely exchanged words at school. I couldn't fathom what she could possibly have to say to me.

'It's great to see you!' Astrid said. 'How have you been? Do you still play the piano?'

I attempted to steer the conversation in a different direction, but she was having none of it.

'Yeah,' she said, 'I've got three kids, can you believe it? But really, I've never forgotten you playing the theme from—'

Surely she could not be serious. I knew what she was going to say, and still I couldn't believe she was actually going to say it.

'You know, the theme from *The Man from Snowy River.* You were fantastic! You still play, don't you?'

In Music classes, waiting for dour Mr Jones to show up, I turned pop-music tricks for my classmates. With the popularity of Billy Joel, Elton John, the theme from *M*A*S*H* and movie soundtracks, the early to mid-1980s were generous to piano players. The song requested most frequently was 'Jessica's Theme' from the 1982 movie *The Man from Snowy River.* The film score was so popular that, more than thirty years later, it remains in Amazon's top fifty soundtracks of that decade. Allegedly 'Jessica's Theme', my signature tune, was partly responsible for a subsequent generation of little Jessicas.

I wasn't the only teenager with a hopeless crush on the film's star, Tom Burlinson, who plays Jim Craig, an intelligent but poorly educated horseman from the remote high country of rural Victoria. He's in love with Jessica, the headstrong daughter of his wealthy landowner boss. Played by Sigrid Thornton, Jessica fulfilled my fantasies of what rebellion against one's parents looked like: to sit at my piano while dreaming of travelling the world, and to retreat each night to my bedroom after a home-cooked meal to read a novel. Jim and Jessica's romance is as practicable as that between any teenagers with little or no income, but I would have had to remove my rose-coloured glasses to see that, and at thirteen mine were affixed permanently to my face.

In the school's political hierarchy I occupied a neutral, if isolated, position. Friendly enough with most of the girls in my year but not a fixed member of any one faction, I was a social Switzerland. Away from the piano, many of the other girls may rarely have given me the time of day, but my ability to reel off popular songs and sight-read—to play a piece of new music at first sight—put me beyond the brunt of their forensic criticism. Because of the piano I enjoyed a level of immunity from the social persecution that the coolest girls perpetrated on other awkward saps who lacked the protection of an instrument.

Twenty years later, I was astounded to realise that despite feeling like the world's biggest nerd at the time, I had earned their admiration and respect even though I could neither see nor enjoy it.

My school reunion turned into a recital of the popular songs I used to play by request before and after Music classes. A chorus of mature women sang out song titles with startling recall: 'Jessica's Theme', the theme from *M★A★S★H* ('Suicide Is Painless') and an Elton John medley. They also remembered me as quite the Billy Joel interpreter, wrapping my still-small hands around 'New York State of Mind' and 'Allentown'. I had played those songs repeatedly, dreaming of living in New York one day when I didn't have to get up at six every morning before school, or rely on my mother to drive me around. I had no idea what a New York state of mind might be, nor where Allentown was, or why they might have been shutting down the factories there. Though I learned that Allentown was in New Jersey, it might as well have been New Zealand for all I understood about the place. Had everyone else been as oblivious as I was to the irony of my performing songs about creative melancholy and job insecurity while in the cloistered protection of a private girls' school?

After *The Man from Snowy River* shot him to stardom, Tom Burlinson acted in several films before carving a successful career from singing and musical theatre, with a specialty in impersonating Frank Sinatra—when I, as a thirteen-year-old with an imperfect understanding of the relationship of one's life to the plans we make for it, had expected him to become a major movie star.

At the reunion, my peers did not see my bookish 37-year-old face but that of the musical teenage girl, frozen in time beside the assembly-hall Steinway. I was as guilty as anyone of fixing in my mind an image of a girl who in many cases bore no relation to the woman in front of me, reeling off her personal and professional statistics as though I was a census collector.

Yet I was struck by the similarities in my peers' life stories. They put me in mind of another famous statement of Joan Didion: 'We tell ourselves stories in order to live.' I learned that a demographically disproportionate number of women had borne three children. That an even higher number lived in the suburb in which they had grown up. And that many had worked for one employer for more than ten years. We tell each other stories in order to live with ourselves, is more like it.

After John died I had yearned to be far away from everything comfortable and familiar to me, so at the reunion I stuck to my story that I had moved to New York after being widowed. But as these conversations confirmed, the truth was, with or without my husband, I never could picture myself living their sort of life. The idea of working at one place for a decade did my head in, as did the idea of moving back to live in Hunters Hill. No wonder they all expected me to still be sitting at the piano. And children? Despite my grief as a young widow, I was quietly relieved John and I had never had a baby. My perception of parenting, forged in a house devoted to routine and repetition, was limited to a daily grind of dirty nappies, endless laundry and thankless meals.

On the other hand, the reunion forced me to see the tangible benefits that accrued from the routines and the repetitions that my former schoolmates described with *wabi-sabi* smiles. A stable income. A family life. Enduring love, or whatever describes the glue that binds a couple after years of childrearing.

I thought of the line about apples not falling far from the tree. I had come to the reunion looking in vain for other apples that had scattered far and wide, and that had suffered a few bruises as a result. My mistake had been to expect difference, not repetition. I now see this was an unintended consequence of my grief, which in its voracious need for disruption had led me to change country, career, and the way I chose to work and relate to people I loved: via Skype. Though the remoteness was largely of my own making, I felt as distant from these women at thirty-seven as I had at seventeen.

Almost everyone I spoke to that night had been certain that I must have been 'doing something with the piano' for the past two decades. To them, I had been working as a musician, not as a book editor. I felt sorry to disappoint them, and bewildered by their surprise at how differently my life had turned out from what they'd expected. Hadn't theirs? Frankly, the way my life had turned out was a surprise to me. I had not planned to be in my late thirties, trying to improvise a life as a widow—and a self-employed one to boot, cobbling together bits and pieces in what has come to be known as the gig economy. That was the only sort of gig I played these days.

My reunion sent me reeling. If I'd been as good a pianist as my peers remembered, why hadn't I become a professional? Why had I let my musicianship lapse after all those years of intensive study and practice? What had been the point of learning to play? And what would my life look like now if I'd pursued sounds instead of sentences? These are the questions that a woman of privilege may ask herself, lying in her parents' spare bedroom on the night before her return flight to New York, because she had an education and a choice in the matter. Regret and self-doubt are the currency of decisions. Twenty years after making mine,

I—like anyone who chooses one path over another—was living with the consequences.

♫

Millions of girls have learned to play the piano over the course of its history, and only relatively recently have gifted women pianists had much say about what to do with their talent. The example of Maria Anna Mozart illustrates the ivory ceiling that many talented women pianists have run into.

In 1763, the eleven-year-old piano prodigy began a lucrative three-year grand tour of Europe with her younger brother, performing duets for stunned audiences of aristocrats from Salzburg to London. Nannerl, as Maria Anna was known, sang and played harpsichord or piano; Wolfgang Amadeus played violin as well as the keyboard instruments. Nannerl's ambitious father Leopold had taught her piano from the age of three, as he began teaching her little brother five years later. When Nannerl was twelve, Leopold declared her to be one of the finest pianists in Europe.[1]

Few female pianists made public performances in the eighteenth century. When they did, it was often because they could be admired as freaks or anomalies, as was blind keyboardist Maria Theresia Paradis when she toured Paris and London.[2] Other performers attracted audiences with the novelty value of being foreign or a child.

But in 1769, despite Nannerl's undeniable gifts, Leopold Mozart decided that his daughter would no longer tour or play for a paying audience. She had reached the marriageable age of eighteen, when the virtue of a musical girl began to hold greater cultural power than her virtuosity. Leopold felt that while it was one thing for his talented child to show off in front of an audience, something was shameful about a grown woman performing in public, irrespective of his pride in her ability. In December 1769, when her father and brother boarded a carriage en route to perform in Italy, Nannerl broke down weeping. She was staying at home, where she would perform the domestic roles that her father had chosen for her, rather than the one she would have chosen herself. She locked herself in her room and did not emerge until the next day.[3]

In what became a common progression for virtuosic women pianists, Nannerl reinvented herself as a highly regarded teacher, following her father's pedagogical path without travelling anywhere. Almost ten years after Mozart's solo career took off, Nannerl was still her father's housekeeper in Salzburg and unmarried, because he had forced her to reject the proposal of the man she loved. Oblivious—or perhaps tone-deaf—to the ways in which his decisions had constrained her personal and professional opportunities, Leopold boasted of his daughter's musicianship in a letter to his brother. 'She can improvise like you wouldn't believe,' he wrote in February 1778, referring to Nannerl's ability to create music spontaneously as she played.[4] By their nature, improvisations are not intended to be written down, so we have no record of Nannerl's. At the age of thirty-two she married a much-older man, a twice-widowed magistrate who brought five children to their union. In a salutary lesson for multi-taskers, Nannerl managed to teach while raising them plus the three that the couple composed together.

In October 1777, Nannerl's brother had travelled to the Bavarian city of Augsburg to meet Johann Stein, whose hand-crafted pianos had impressed the composer. During Mozart's visit, Stein's eight-year-old daughter, Nanette, performed for him. As a precocious virtuosa, she was accustomed to public performance, but not to criticism of the sort that Mozart offered her father—which he recorded in a letter to his own father:

> Mr Stein is completely silly about his daughter. She is eight years old and learns everything only from memory. She might amount to something, she has genius; but . . . she will get nowhere, she will never get much speed, because she makes a special effort to make her hand heavy. She will never get what is the most needful and the hardest, and the principal thing in music, Tempo, because from infancy on she has made it a point not to play in time.[5]

Tempo, the speed at which a piece of music should be played, is one of the key paradoxes of musicianship: the more time the young pianist devotes to playing in tempo, which is to say at a consistent speed—even if that speed is as slow as a wet week—the faster she will be able to play, as her dexterity catches up with her impatience. In Mozart's identification of Nanette Stein's tendency to rush, predilection for memorising the notes and heavy wrist, he could have been writing about any number of the thousands of young girls learning to play the piano in the late eighteenth century, or in the late nineteenth, or even the late twentieth—myself included.

In 1792, when Johann Stein died, 23-year-old Nanette took over her father's business. Who knows if she heeded any of Mozart's advice about technique, but by then she knew more than anyone about the mechanics of building pianos. She was clearly entrepreneurial too, because she shifted the family business to Vienna—where there was a burgeoning demand for instruments—and in 1794 established herself as the managing director of a new business under her married name, referencing her father: Nanette Streicher, née Stein. Hers was effectively one of the first piano factories. Stein's handcrafted output had been approximately seventeen pianos per year, but Nanette's operation produced forty-nine to fifty-three in the same time.[6]

Because of Nanette Streicher's expertise and business acumen, the piano was on its way into the homes of aristocrats and the wealthiest merchants in Europe as a coveted piece of domestic furniture. And as with any high-end product, emerging technology soon liberated the piano from exclusivity. Before long, thanks to factories such as Nanette's popping up across Europe and the United States, production increased to meet the demand of the burgeoning Victorian middle classes. By 1847, according to Arthur Loesser's comprehensive *Men, Women and Pianos: A Social History*, 60,000 instruments were manufactured each year in Paris alone, and 20,000 in England. Within a few decades of its invention, the piano had become 'the social anchor of the middle-class home'.[7] As it had for Nannerl Mozart, the piano shaped Nanette's life, but possibly in a different way from what she had imagined as a child. She was significant in the history of talented women pianists because she turned her musicianship into a thriving business that ushered in generations of girls at the piano from all social classes.

As the product equally of art and commerce, the piano walked hand in hand with the Industrial Revolution. In its large-scale production, the instrument was one of the first consumer items to face competition from rival nations.

Annual production worldwide increased almost tenfold in the second half of the nineteenth century; by 1910 it was 500,000. But despite the piano's cutting-edge relationship to technology and manufacturing, playing the instrument was seen as a recreation for girls rather than boys. The 1881 *Girls Own Annual* included an advice column on how to purchase and look after your piano.[8] In his bizarre best-seller, the 1871 spiritual-musical manifesto *Music and Morals*, the Reverend H.R. Haweis spuriously maintains that 'the piano makes a girl sit upright and pay attention to details', whereas Latin grammar strengthens a boy's memory.[9] I'm not sure if the good reverend ever tried learning a Mozart sonata by heart. Posture aside, I well remember that effort as an intensive and repetitive combination of attention to detail and memorisation.

Not everyone perceived the ubiquity of pianos in domestic life as an altogether happy event. 'All—except perhaps teachers of music—will agree that at the present day the piano is too much with us,' declared the *British Medical Journal* in April 1899. Protesting the 'scandalous waste of time, money and labour' of music lessons for most piano students, the *Journal* insisted that 'an ordinary intelligent girl will learn half the languages of Europe in the time given to her abortive struggles with an art she really does not care for and cannot understand'.[10]

Whether or not this judgement was true, the piano lost its central place in domestic life after World War I. Presented with the gramophone, the pianola and expanding economic opportunities for women, many ordinary intelligent girls found other things to do. By 1977, the year I began learning the instrument, French philosopher Roland Barthes was asking: 'Who plays the piano today?'[11] In 'Musica Practica', the essay that poses the question, Barthes describes the decline in amateur musicianship as only an amateur musician can: with nostalgia and indignation. 'Initially the province of the idle (aristocratic) class, it lapsed into an insipid social rite with the coming of the democracy of the bourgeoisie (the piano, the young lady, the drawing room, the nocturne), and then faded out altogether,' he writes. His potted history has a large hole in it the size of millions of working-class families, who embraced the piano as a ticket to respectability in the second half of the nineteenth century.

While thousands of upper middle-class girls may have been playing nocturnes in drawing rooms for prospective husbands, working-class families caused the explosion in demand when upright pianos became available mid-century. The upright is easier to fit into a room than a grand piano, and much cheaper. And to accommodate families aspiring to acquire one, piano makers invented the payment system of hire-purchase, meaning that the instrument was the first product to be sold by this method. Those without the means to pay in full at the time of ordering could take delivery for a deposit and then make a series of monthly repayments until they owned their piano outright. The system proved so successful that by 1892 hire-purchase comprised 70 per cent of all piano sales.[12] In *Women in Love*, D.H. Lawrence gets close to the truth, which is to say the symbolism, of piano ownership, when he writes of the 'amazing heights of upright grandeur' provided by a piano in the home of a coalminer: 'It makes him so much higher in his neighbouring collier's eyes. He sees himself reflected in the neighbouring opinion . . . several feet taller on the strength of the pianoforte, and he is satisfied.'

The pleasure of playing the piano knows boundaries of neither class nor technique. In 'Musica Practica', the bourgeois Barthes distinguishes the music we listen to from the 'practical music' that we play at home as amateurs who 'inscribe' it on our bodies while we transmit sound and meaning from page to instrument. In Barthes' case he inscribed mostly Schumann, which he played every morning for his mother—with whom he lived for sixty years. We may physically inscribe our music through touch and sight and hearing as we play, as Barthes says, but we also inscribe it on our bodies when we're not playing, in the memories and associations—positive and negative—we form with music and take through life.

At the most literal level, amateur pianists tend to play as adults the music they learned as children, not straying far in terms of repertoire from those individual works that loom disproportionately large in their imagination. Jane Austen, who was born in 1775, was a diligent piano student. She practised every morning before nine, when she prepared a breakfast of tea and toast for her father and the rest of the family.[13] The last quarter of the eighteenth century was a time when Beethoven was composing and Mozart famous, but they don't make it into her novels. Jane's heroines perform works by Haydn, Hoffmeister, Pleyel and Sterkel—composers whose music she learned as a teenager.[14] As a piano student, my holy trinity was Bach, Mozart and Beethoven. In the same way that we are what we eat, we become whom we play. The principle holds true for the professional as well as the amateur musician.

Amateur. It's a French word that comes from the Italian *amatore*, which itself descends from the Latin *amator*, or lover. In the coy phrasing of the OED, an amateur is someone who is 'fond of something' or who 'has a taste for something'. But fondness seems a rather pastel version of love to me. When I hear the word *lover* it's painted in bold primary colours, conjuring messy bedsheets, open mouths, a reward worth vigorous effort. It's passion, not fondness, that drives the amateur football teams, the needlepoint obsessives, the mobile-phone photographers, the community theatre junkies and the garage bands. The amateur is the person who chooses to spend time practising the thing they love—and more often than not, they're doing it without hope or expectation of monetary reward, an attitude that today is increasingly regarded with suspicion if not downright hostility. The person who pursues a passion without a plan to 'monetise' the skill or knowledge is considered foolish rather than wise. In its adjectival form, *amateur* is defined by contrast with *professional*, which is all about getting paid. As a result, the amateur is associated with a lack of skill.

♫

What the women at my high school reunion did not know was that, having experienced a spectacular failure, I had concluded that I would not—more definitively, could not—become a professional musician. After an adolescence characterised by intensive practice and regular public performance, I had all but renounced my love of the piano. Ever since, I had felt ashamed of being an amateur and could not enjoy playing for its own sake. I had given up all performance opportunities and come to loathe anyone listening to me play; I heard only the gulf between how I used to be able to play, when I practised for hours every day, and how I played now.

After the reunion, I was tormented by the suspicion that I had made a profound mistake. Though I had lived with a keyboard or an upright piano nearby for most of my adult life, my playing mostly felt half-hearted. When I moved to New York in 2006, there was no longer even a wobbly keyboard in my apartment. Widowhood had made me feel as isolated as I had as an adolescent, hiding in plain sight at the piano in an auditorium full of my peers. Two decades later, the reunion made me suspect that my early dedication to the piano had shaped my life in ways I had not fully understood, and that by cutting myself off from the instrument, I had lost something. After years of self-enforced hibernation, the reunion forced me to recognise that I yearned to connect again—with other people, and with the piano.

♫

In 1840, the composer and piano teacher Carl Czerny published *Letters to a Young Lady, on the Art of Playing the Pianoforte, from the earliest rudiments to the highest state of cultivation.* The ideal piano student of the nineteenth century was a marriageable young woman from a respectable family, and at the time of the book's publication, thousands of them were actively—if not all enthusiastically—learning to play.

Famous as one of Beethoven's star pupils, Czerny was a natural self-promoter. The previous year he had published the four-volume *Great Pianoforte School*, modestly describing it as 'beyond all comparison the most extensive and complete method for that instrument ever published'. My mother often told me that self-praise is no recommendation, but Czerny's chutzpah only fanned the flames of his reputation as a teacher. In *Letters to a Young Lady* he identified an untapped market—young girls who are studying the piano; or, to be more precise, their paying parents—and his fame spread.

Czerny addresses his ten-part correspondence to an imaginary beginner named Cecilia whom he fantasises to be a 'talented and well-educated girl of about twelve years old, residing at a distance in the country'. Cecilia's upper-class parents—who supported her acquisition of keyboard skills as a tactical advantage in the years-long battle to snare an eligible bachelor—agreed with Czerny that 'pianoforte playing, though suitable to every one, is yet more particularly one of the most charming and honourable accomplishments for young ladies'.[15] By the time Czerny capitalised on it, this shtick had been around for nearly a century. In his *Encyclopédie*, a series of volumes published between 1751 and 1777, the philosopher and critic Denis Diderot listed piano-playing as 'one of the primary ornaments in the education of women'. The belief was so prevalent that in the 1830s, mass-market reproductions of female music-makers were as widely available as prints of Robert Doisneau's photograph *The Kiss* today. For the Cecilias of the world, their amateur musicianship was as ornamental as the pianos themselves, expensive luxury items of domestic furniture that signified wealth and social status.

In 1774, Goethe's lovesick hero in *The Sorrows of Young Werther* was so carried away by his passion for pianist Charlotte that he decided suicide was the only way out of his torment. But a century on, the Victorians made an art out of portraying the piano as an outlet for emotional girls. Edmond de Goncourt described the piano as 'the lady's hashish', while the Reverend Haweis' bestseller *Music and Morals* went through sixteen printings, purchased by parents and pastors horrified at the release of pent-up feelings that had no other channel for their expression. In its critical diagnosis, the *British Medical Journal* attributed to piano practice the 'chloroses and neuroses from which so many young girls suffer', turning the human primal responsiveness to music into gendered pathology.

The girl sitting at a piano was such a potent cultural theme that it was often caricatured. In 1880, the French illustrator and cartoonist Draner drew a woman playing the piano with her right hand, while stirring a pot on the stove with her left.[16] The truth of this visual joke was that most girl pianists in the late nineteenth century were not budding minor aristocrats like Cecilia, but daughters of the working class like my grandmother Alice, who was born in Glasgow in 1895—girls who grew up knowing how to play the wooden spoons as well as the piano.

3

When she smiled, my grandmother revealed a perfect set of false teeth the colour of old piano keys. But she deployed her smile unexpectedly, as an assassin might a concealed weapon. She lived at a place known as One Tree Point, on what in the late 1970s constituted the south-western fringe of Sydney. I dreaded having to visit her. Our epic journeys from Hunters Hill took place on the occasional Sundays when my father made us pancakes for breakfast, as if the sugar sprinkles would sweeten the lemon juice of that long car trip, and longer visit, still ahead.

I glanced at my mother across the kitchen table to read her face. She always sat in the same position, the north to my south. To be geographically accurate it was the other way around, but my sense of direction was then as undeveloped as the rest of me. From the way my mother briefly pressed her eyes closed and remained tight-lipped, I knew that she didn't want to go either. Of my mother's silence I heard every note.

After what felt like two hours we parked outside my grandmother's self-contained cottage, one in a row of identical blood-red brick dwellings. It wasn't far from the Padstow water tower, which looked like a UFO that had been covered in concrete to hide the bleeding obvious. My grandmother's relocation from Yeoval, a small town in the central-west of New South Wales, had not been by choice. My younger brother and I clambered out of my father's car. Arriving meant we were closer to the halfway point of our round trip.

Alice Lloyd opened her front door and stepped onto the tiny concrete landing. Despite her scuffed house slippers and her flesh-coloured pantyhose, thick enough to floss with, she effected a regal air. She waited for us to ascend the four steps to greet her, with the solemnity of Queen Elizabeth standing on the terrace at Buckingham Palace.

'Go on, say hello,' Dad said, urging me along the path towards her. At the car my brother clung like static to my mother's skirt.

On the landing I stood on tiptoe to give the old lady a kiss. When she brushed her lips against my cheek they didn't purse together or make any sound. Her greyish-white whiskers tickled as I inhaled the tobacco on her clothes. Instead of a hug she gripped my shoulder with one hand so that I could feel each bony finger. She scared the hell out of me, but I had no choice but to follow her inside, where the kettle was invariably on.

By the time the rest of my family joined us, a pot of tea ensconced inside a crocheted cosy sat on the kitchen table like a caffeinated Trojan horse. 'I'll be Mother,' Alice said, standing to pour the strong black tea into floral-patterned china cups.

As Alice handed them out, each cup trembling slightly in its matching saucer, my eyes locked on her stained fingertips. Dad had explained that their dull mustard-yellow tinge was because she rolled her own cigarettes, but I didn't understand why you would waste time rolling cigarettes if your aim was to smoke them.

'Tell Granny your news,' Dad prompted.

Embarrassed, I said, 'I started learning the piano.' There was no piano inside her cottage, even though Dad was always telling me how his mother had taught piano when he was a child. And I knew my father was adopted, so it wasn't as if I was carrying on a family tradition by learning to play. But I could hardly bear to disappoint my parents. They had been married for eleven years before I showed up. From the moment of my late arrival, my job was to be agreeable at all times.

'The pianner?' Granny's bushy white eyebrows shot up above her thick glasses. 'That's good,' she said, firing off an unexpected smile. She took a sip of tea and sucked at her false teeth. 'You know, the most important thing is to practise.'

A ticking wall clock punctuated the uncomfortable quiet that descended. Economy was a defining principle of conversation around the dinner table at home, and I understood there would be nothing further now. My father smiled at me and gave my leg a reassuring pat. He was disappointed, but perhaps not surprised. Neither he nor his sister, my aunt Charlotte, could play the piano. Their mother had taught other people's children, but not her own.

When Alice died eighteen months later, in the winter of 1978, Dad took us on a long road trip to Yeoval. Those approaching via the Great Western Highway encountered a sign that announced the entrance to 'The Greatest Little Town in the West'. Even then I regarded the claim with scepticism. The giveaways were the bullet holes riddling the metal placard and the absence of people. Long tufts of sun-bleached grass waved from lonely crossroads. Dilapidated wooden fences enclosed paddocks of wheat. The doors of a miniature weatherboard church were padlocked in a gesture more hopeful than defensive, with the most recent estimate of Yeoval's population a tiny 293. The town resembled the abandoned set of a B-grade western.

Yeoval's sole claim to fame is as the place where Andrew Barton Paterson, better known as Banjo, spent his first five years in the late 1860s. He grew up on Buckinbah Station, a sprawling property that named the original township. In

1882, when Buckinbah was renamed as Yeoval, the young Paterson was working as an articled clerk for a Sydney law firm as a recent graduate of the prestigious Sydney Grammar School. It was another three years before poems under the name 'Banjo' began appearing in the *Bulletin*, which first published his best-known work, 'The Man from Snowy River', in 1890.

Adopted soon after his birth in 1934, my father grew up on a small wheat farm amid plagues and drought, with loving parents who pinched every penny. He made his pocket money by skinning rabbits. At times, he said, so many rabbits covered the ground that 'it looked like the earth had got up and walked'. Eventually his family left the farm and moved into a single-storey dwelling in Yeoval proper, where his father George Lloyd took over a stock and station agency selling everything from farming machinery to fresh eggs.

From the back seat of my father's car I stared at the forlorn weatherboard house, for which modest was too modest a word. In summer they must have baked like bread inside it. The house looked both authentic and makeshift, like a forgotten display in a museum of disappointment. I could hardly conceive of anyone, let alone my father, living in it—or turning up on its drab doorstep for a piano lesson with my terrifying grandmother. It wasn't much, but to Alice I suppose it hadn't been much for more than thirty years.

Between my mother's general impatience with my father's trip down memory lane and my ongoing sibling skirmish in the back seat, we did not dwell long on the sorry sight. Owing to the heat, the dust, the sense of desolation, and my horror at Dad's stories of rabbits and locusts, it was on that rural tour that I came to associate living in the country with the Old Testament.

A few years ago I found myself once again travelling with my parents to visit an elderly woman on the outskirts of Sydney. This time it was my aunt Charlotte, my father's sister, who lived on the city's rural fringe. Over three decades, undulating fields where sheep and cattle had safely grazed had become purpose-built enclaves of identical single-level houses on quarter-acre blocks. We sat down before the pot of tea that remained as essential at family gatherings as the cup of wine at Communion. We had just returned from a visit to the house next door, where my sixty-year-old cousin Bronwyn, Charlotte's daughter, lived alone. In an architectural echo of the notion that women grow up to look like their mothers, the two houses were exactly the same on the outside, though their interiors differed in layout. The collective glassy stare of my cousin's porcelain dolls, which sat in rows on her living room wall, gave me the creeps. They looked like something out of a horror movie—the replication of a notion of beauty from an era when an intact hymen and the ability to play the piano, rather than a trust fund and an MBA from Harvard, represented ultimate social value. Rosy-cheeked maidens sat shoulder to shoulder in long silk dresses of block pink, lemon, mauve and the inevitable white. All dressed up and nowhere to go, they gazed into a future that would never materialise.

Sipping my tea at Charlotte's, I couldn't decide which was more distressing: the size of Bronwyn's doll collection, or the fact that she lived next door to her parents.

Toward the end of the first cup, Charlotte leaned on wobbly knees and slowly stood up from the table. 'I've got something to show you,' she said as she ambled in the direction of her sewing room. In years gone by this sort of threat announced the imminent bestowing of a home-made tapestry to hide in a drawer when I got home. Now in her late eighties, my aunt had discovered the internet and enthused ad taedium about branches of the family tree she had collected during her genealogical research. The room that had once been dedicated to sewing and painting-by-numbers was now the headquarters of Charlotte's investigations.

To my surprise, my aunt returned clutching a bundle of documents relating to her mother's musicianship. In April 1912, at the age of sixteen, Alice May Morrison Taylor attained her Elementary Certificate by passing examinations in Musical Memory, in Time, in Tune and in Sight Singing, then the Intermediate level just five months later. In florid script the Intermediate Certificate announces that Alice has fulfilled the Tonic Sol-Fa College of Glasgow's requirements for Reading Music at First Sight, and Writing it from Ear, and of eligibility for an advanced Choir. In between these achievements, she passed her First Grade examinations in

Staff Notation (the ability to write music) in May 1912, and claimed her Elementary Certificate in Theory of Music the following January. There were references to her public appearances and letters of recommendation for her employment as a choir mistress. 'She is a very painstaking and enthusiastic musician and I have great pleasure in recommending her for any important appointment she may seek,' wrote her teacher, the esteemed local musician Frederick Hervey, less than two years later. Alice had been a late bloomer but a fast learner.

I found it difficult to believe that the subject of these certificates and glowing recommendations was the same woman who, one decade on, battled rabbit plagues and endless dust on a wheat farm in the middle of Nowhere, New South Wales. It was impossible to reconcile the evidence of a very musical girl with the family story of a humourless woman with a matching chip on each shoulder. With the wife who recorded local marriages on her kitchen calendar so she could determine, by the birthdate of the couple's firstborn, which weddings had been shotgun. With the mother who delighted in the Christmas gift of a cardigan from her son until she discovered that her daughter-in-law had selected it, when it became unsuitable and had to be returned to David Jones.

In an effort to prompt kinder memories of my grandmother, I dug out some old photo albums from the closet in my parents' house that served as the family archive. The Alice pickings proved to be slim. A couple of fading colour snaps from the 1970s capture her as a kind of human scarecrow, all fuzzy grey hair and rakish frame.

One of them depicts the two of us mid-slide on the uncomfortable black leather couch in the living room of the house I grew up in. Alice is wearing a blue and white floral print dress, and black old-lady rubber lace-up shoes—which, apart from the house slippers, were the only things I saw on her feet. I'm in a signature sprawl, one matchstick leg flung out in front of me and the other over the side, a book in my left hand and my right thumb in my mouth. Between us lies the naked body of my doll, Gail.

Gail was an unlikely gift from one of my father's acquaintances in the building trade. Until I met her I had exhibited no interest in dolls, but I had fallen hard. Wherever I went, Gail went too—including a swimming pool, which transformed her black nylon tresses into a triangular lump. Soon after that, her head was somehow divorced from her torso, so she became less than half the doll she had been; in an enduring family mystery, her body was never seen again. Gail's dismemberment only made me love her more. Her head accompanied me everywhere. At night I spread out her matted inky halo on my pillow and laid my own head of thick brown hair upon it. I loved feeling those soft acrylic lumps against the cool silkiness of my hair. Lying in bed, my face pressed up against Gail, was the only time when my hair was free. My mother loathed freely flowing locks on any woman, but particularly on her daughter. She insisted that my hair be harnessed in either a ponytail or pigtails so tight that they never had to be redone.

In the photograph Gail was yet to lose her torso. It's my only photo of her intact, and until recently its primary value was as the poignant Before shot of my beloved confidante. Looking at the picture again, I noticed a lot of space between my grandmother and me on that couch. Who can say whether she had been reading to me or if I had been trying to read to her—or perhaps to Gail.

Reading is something I associate with my mother, who drove me every week to the Gladesville Public Library to replenish my Holly Hobbie drawstring book bag; who read stories to me until I grew old enough to read them for myself; who volunteered to help other children at my school learn to read. Who, though she was in an almost constant orbit, shuttling between the kitchen and laundry, the clothesline and the bedroom, the school and the supermarket, could always be found, in her rare moments of stillness, with a magazine or newspaper in her hands.

Because of my intense attachment to Gail I identified strongly with Christopher Robin's utter dependence on Pooh in *When We Were Very Young* and *Now We Are Six*, which my mother had bought for me and which I obsessively read and re-read. It wasn't only the rhymes of the poems and their exotic locations that enchanted me. Christopher's melancholy sang to me from the creamy illustrated pages, and I longed for the kind of solitude in which a poem might present itself for me to write down. In A.A. Milne's world, children visited Buckingham Palace and scolded their nanny and sat quietly on their favourite step. No one interrupted their daydreaming to ask what they were doing or to remind them that dinner would be ready soon. How marvellous to write poetry like Christopher, I would think. But no sooner had I started down that path than I tripped over a large stumbling block that seemed impassable: what would I possibly write about? I had no step of my own, no nanny, and no chance of visiting Buckingham Palace. Who would be interested in poems about a little girl and her best friend, Gail? And with Gail now just a head with matted black hair, any hypothetical illustrations would have been a sticking point, too.

My favourite books featured a heroine solving a mystery. The escapades of Enid Blyton's Famous Five and Secret Seven. The neighbourhood adventures of Milly-Molly-Mandy. The Nancy Drew detective stories by Carolyn Keene, Julie Campbell Tatham's tales starring Trixie Belden, and later Agatha Christie's elderly sleuth Miss Marple. Together they formed a genealogy of investigative heroines. The puzzles they encountered were inevitably solved by the last page. Their every story had a positive ending; every problem, a neat solution.

But now, as I reviewed the certificates and correspondence relating to my grandmother's musicianship, I realised that Alice's story remained a mystery to me. What had happened to lead her in the opposite direction—geographically and professionally—of the one in which she'd seemed headed? Why had she given up a burgeoning professional life in music in Glasgow? How could she pack up her talent and experience and sail to Australia, only to settle for life on a farm?

Was my grandmother's altered relationship to music a result of financial circumstances, boredom, disappointment—or something else? Had the relentless Australian sun bleached her of her passion for singing? If not, where did she channel her emotional attachment to music? What did it mean to lead an early life in which music had been central, only to give it up like an impossible love? I had done this myself, throwing away thirteen years of intensive piano study for a professional life that had no music in it. What had each of us gained in doing so—and what had we lost?

My grandmother's brief career in music was a tantalising and inexplicable development. The few odd pieces of Alice's puzzle that I possessed formed no coherent picture;

instead, they created a portrait defined by what was missing. Suddenly I felt pulled toward Alice by what little I knew and an urgent desire to find other parallels between our experiences as musical girls. I wanted to use her scant biographical record to explore these parallels, and the ways in which our experiences reflected those of other girls drawn from the pages of history and fiction—aristocrats and spinsters, entrepreneurs and writers—who had sat at the piano over the course of its history. I came to believe that setting aside Alice's frightening mask of old age might help me to understand my own voyage around the piano—and help me to find my way back.

4

MY FIRST PIANO WAS A BABY GRAND. I loved the instrument's glossy black lid, the clink of its metal keys, and the way it was light enough for me to tuck under my left arm. It would definitely have been the left arm because at five years of age I sucked my right thumb with a degree of attachment that not even my favourite toy could compete with. *Security Is a Thumb and a Blanket*, according to *Peanuts* comic-strip creator Charles Schulz's book of the same name. There must have been something to his claim because the book outsold two volumes on the John F. Kennedy assassination to become the second biggest-selling book of 1963.[17] But blankets were for babies. For me, security was a thumb and a miniature piano.

The only toy pianist—or any kind of pianist—of my acquaintance was Charlie Brown's friend Schroeder. We seemed to be around the same age but judging by his technical facility Schroeder must have started playing as soon as he emerged from the womb. I was encouraged that he could produce such exquisite music from his instrument, because it was exactly the same shape, colour and dimensions as mine. He was so good that he hardly ever referred to printed music and never needed to practise, and yet he practised all the time. It was from the blond boy-genius that I learned to crouch at my toy piano: back bent over, shoulders hunched up around my ears, legs crossed, fingers dropping from my hands held high and close together like pedigree paws.

Schroeder's appearances were the second-best thing about the *Peanuts* comics and television specials, which I watched sitting on the olive-brown linoleum floor, Gail's decapitated head in my lap and my thumb in my mouth. Above Schroeder's voluminous golden hair a series of black squiggles and lines and symbols sometimes materialised. Despite having never seen written music before, I understood that somehow the lines and dots represented the sounds that Schroeder produced at his toy piano. Did he know what each dot and line meant? How had he learned that? I watched Schroeder's little fingers chase each other all over the keys as the score—which Charles Schulz faithfully transcribed—keeps pace with him, one or two bars at a time. It seemed both beautiful and incredibly difficult.

If Schroeder's taste had mirrored Schulz's, we would associate the child prodigy with a love of Brahms. But for the purposes of the cartoon strip, 'Beethoven was funnier,' he admitted.[18]

Lying on his back on the piano lid, Snoopy reaches up to plant a big kiss on Schroeder's nose. 'You never know how Beethoven is going to affect someone,' he says.

Schroeder wasn't alone in respecting the emotive potential of Beethoven's music. Lenin listened to the 'Appassionata' piano sonata number 23 every day, though he thought it was too much of a distraction. He famously walked out of a performance of the work, saying, 'If I keep listening to Beethoven's *Appassionata*, I won't be able to finish the revolution.'[19]

Leo Tolstoy suspected that Beethoven's virtuosic 'Kreutzer' sonata for piano and violin could arouse a murderous passion. In 1889 Tolstoy wrote out his fear in the novella *The Kreutzer Sonata*, in which the narrator Pozdnyshev murders his accompanist wife out of jealousy over her musical relationship with the male violinist while they rehearse and perform that work.

Happily in the world of *Peanuts*, all Schroeder had to worry about was the unwanted attention of Lucy van Pelt. In the stage play *You're a Good Man, Charlie Brown*, Lucy confesses to Schroeder while he plays Beethoven's 'Moonlight' sonata that it's always been her dream to marry someone who plays the piano. As soon as he reaches the end, he frowns at Lucy and walks away. I couldn't blame him—why any little girl would be thinking about getting married was beyond me. When Lucy replaces Schroeder's portrait of Beethoven with a framed picture of herself, Schroeder goes berserk. He may be able to 'save . . . himself from everyday neuroses by sublimating them in a lofty form of artistic madness', as Umberto Eco has suggested,[20] but he could not play Lucy away. Undaunted, she shrugs, remembering the wise words of her aunt Marion, who told her, 'Never try to discuss marriage with a musician.'

Watching these child-adults as a child, I was exasperated by Lucy's refusal to leave Schroeder alone to practise. How could you improve with someone like her around? All she ever wanted to do was go outside and play. Schroeder knew that to be an excellent pianist you had to do it alone, without anyone bothering you, spend lots of time practising, and not worry that you were missing out on anything. Schroeder was my introduction to the physical and social isolation necessary to become an instrumental virtuoso.

From Monday through Saturday the talkback radio presenters shouted in the background of our family life like angry gods, but for one morning each week my mother allowed the *wireless*, as she called it, to be switched off. My parents obeyed their day of rest with their own rituals of words and music.

My mother pored over one of the two home-delivered Sunday papers at the kitchen table, beginning with the personal classifieds, a section she dubbed *Hatches, Matches, Catches and Dispatches*. She would proceed to read the news of a total stranger's death, or a summary of the most gruesome murder or severe prison sentence, in crisp syllables at maximum volume, for the benefit of my father in the next room, who read the other newspaper from the sports pages forward. He sat in a chair in easy reach of the record player, wearing a fresh pair of KingGee work shorts and a white singlet. His location reflected a rare period of leisure, but his outfit announced his imminent deployment to outstanding tasks around the house. My father's crossed legs, with their knobbly knees and tapping feet, were the first things I saw when I emerged from my bedroom. The blue veins protruded from his pale calves like a relief map of Australia's east coast. The tabloid newspaper in his hands obscured the rest of him, but the angle of its open pages revealed his degree of progress from the back page with the accuracy of a sundial.

There was no rest for the record player on Sunday mornings, though each week my father's musical lesson comprised a different text. Sometimes it was the yee-ha banjo business of John Denver's 'Grandma's Feather Bed'; at others, the rambling anecdotes of Tom T. Hall or Willie Nelson. Either way, I woke up to a story in music whether I wanted to or not. Of Dad's Sunday morning singer-songwriters I unconsciously favoured the British: melancholy Ralph McTell, who mourned the homeless of 'The Streets of London', and the wordy Gilbert O'Sullivan's rhyming nasal twang. In his enthusiasm, my father often attempted to engage me in music appreciation while I still had sleep in my eyes. Decades would pass before he slept later than 7 a.m. 'You can sleep when you're dead,' he'd say. He expected me to be alert from the moment I was vertical. 'Johnny Cash: listen!' he'd say, lowering the newspaper, and I would hear immediately that he had left his teeth in the glass jar in the bathroom. Without them Dad's enunciation was less than perfect, especially when he attempted a mouthful of sibilants: 'In this song he's singing about a boy named Sue.' Out of a fear of disappointing my father, I expressed more enthusiasm for Johnny Cash's throat-lozenge growl than I sometimes felt.

Dad's favourite sound of all was a big band in full swing. Nelson Riddle and the Dorsey Brothers often performed for us on Sunday mornings. Operatic singing might have been likened to the strains of a drowning cat, but the scat singing of Ella Fitzgerald was considered genius. And Sinatra was only ever referred to as Frank. Those musicians known outside our house for breaching the wall between classical and jazz music only performed one style inside it. I heard Benny Goodman play Duke Ellington but not the Mozart clarinet concerto. Instead of Rachmaninov, George Gershwin performed 'Rhapsody in Blue' for us. For years Leonard Bernstein was beloved to me not as a conductor but as the composer of *West Side Story.* My knowledge of 'classical music' was limited to the orchestral soundtrack of Walt Disney's *Fantasia.* There were no 'classical music' records in my house. I didn't know that Beethoven was a composer of 'classical music', and I wasn't familiar with the term 'classical music' or any of the myriad ways in which grown-ups discourage curiosity by naming things and placing them in clearly marked boxes.

The first time I heard Beethoven at home was when Schroeder played the 'Pathétique' and 'Moonlight' sonatas in the *Peanuts* television specials broadcast in Australia during the early 1970s. To sit at those black and white keys helped Schroeder escape real life while keeping completely still; to disappear without leaving the house; to explore pretty sounds that were pure and abstract and free from the world of baseball and Christmas and neighbours like Lucy who didn't understand his passion and dedication. He played in an attitude of joyful self-improvement, looking up to Beethoven who watched over him from the lid of his piano. But Schroeder didn't play simply to get better at playing: his virtuosity was tied to a deep emotional need, and this magical connection to the instrument fascinated me. For as long as his fingers touched the keys in exquisite isolation, Schroeder found relief from frustration, anxiety and distress—emotions I was yet to name.

In the early 1970s the 'Moonlight' sonata was just as popular as it had been after its composition in 1801, and it was one of the first melodies I played by ear on my toy piano. But Beethoven wasn't too happy about its runaway success. 'Surely I've written better things,' he later told Czerny.[21]

Over time I came to realise that of the music I heard during the *Peanuts* specials, Schroeder's Beethoven recitals weren't my favourite. What I enjoyed best were the jaunty soundtracks. Free of any music terminology to name what I heard, my young ears felt an intense affinity for the syncopated swing, the pretty melodies and the minor-sevenths. I thrilled to the walking bass, and the tap and swoosh of the brushes over the drums. Most of all, the miracle of the piano—by turns happy, wistful, ecstatic, morose, hopeful, lonely, impatient—somehow encompassed a whole world of feeling: not just how Charlie Brown or Snoopy or Lucy or Schroeder felt, but how I felt while watching them. It was the piano music that helped me to know how I felt about what I saw—and somehow made me feel it more intensely. How did the music do that? And would it be possible for me to learn how to play such music?

Despite admiring Schroeder's virtuosity and dedication to practice, even then I could tell that his passionate attachment to Beethoven was at the expense of other kinds of music. In that attitude, too, he reflected the ambivalence of his creator towards the music that came to define the sound of the *Peanuts* specials. 'I think jazz is awful,' Schulz told a journalist only months after agreeing to mix traditional hymns with jazz music for the first special, *A Charlie Brown Christmas*, which aired in December 1965. More than ten years earlier, in the strip for 9 December 1952, Charlie Brown interrupts Schroeder while he's playing the 'Moonlight' sonata to ask, 'How about a little jazz?' Schroeder pokes out his tongue and looks physically ill. When Lucy arrives in the final panel, Charlie explains, 'Just the mention of the word is enough to make him shudder.'[22] We can't help how we respond to certain types of music, and on the subject of jazz, Schroeder and I had to agree to disagree. Between my father's record collection and the *Peanuts* soundtrack, I was hooked for life.

♫

My mother stood behind me plaiting my hair while I sat on one of the kitchen table chairs turned sideways, trying hard to stay still. I was about to attend my first live jazz concert with my father, who had bought us tickets to see the Jacques Loussier Trio perform on its 1976 Australasian tour. Mum preferred crooners—like Andy Williams singing

'Moon River'—to the jazz instrumentalists we were going to see, and was staying home to look after my brother.

As usual, there wasn't a single strand of hair on my six-year-old head in doubt of its place. Everyone had to be able to *see my face.* I never understood how my face was obscured by my hair hanging loose to my shoulders—I could see the faces of other girls with long hair very clearly. But the display of abundant hair, without any attempt made to control it, was deeply troubling to my mother. Tucking my hair behind my ears was insufficient.

'Pull your hair back,' she'd say to the parade of glamorous strangers who graced our television screen. At night, topping and tailing green beans into her giant silver colander while she watched, she would yell at actresses and newsreaders. 'Look at that hair. It's a mess. Why doesn't she chop it off?' Hair had to be secured with elastic bands, with braiding, with patience. Even on the rare occasions when I wore my hair down it was still partially up, its front locks restrained by a barrette that, as far as Mum was concerned, represented the only thing standing between her daughter and chaos. I was relieved these women couldn't hear her; I was used to it but suspected others might find her opinions a bit extreme.

My mother wore her straight hair short but permed, in a style that required a maintenance visit to the hairdresser every Wednesday morning. But it never occurred to me to question why I had long hair, nor why cutting it was out of the question.

♫

My father and I walked up the broad and shallow steps from George Street to the main entrance of the Sydney Town Hall. Inside, hundreds of women's shoes clicked as they walked across the white marble floor, though my polished round-tipped Clarks made no sound. After ascending a staircase that led to the balcony, we sat about a third of the way down one of the long sides of the rectangular auditorium. I stood up to peer over the edge—our row was close to it—and stared at all the grown bodies filling the seats below us. I was short for my age and understood, as my father must have when reserving the tickets, that I wouldn't see anything of the concert if I were trying to look over the heads of several hundred adults. On the stage I saw an enormous grand piano, a double bass lying on its side, and a drum kit shaped like a cresting wave. I thought of Schroeder and Snoopy's combo.

The central dilemma of the *Peanuts* TV special *Play It Again, Charlie Brown* is whether or not Lucy and Charlie can convince Schroeder that 'it's all right to play some modern music'. Having secured Schroeder his first gig, Lucy is distraught when Peppermint Patty forbids him from playing Beethoven. Instead he's to play with the 'combo', which consists of scruffy Pig-Pen at the drums, Charlie on the acoustic guitar, and Snoopy playing 'walking bass' by climbing all over the gigantic instrument. When Schroeder discovers the combo jamming on a bluesy syncopated number, he is so disgusted he mimes a gag reflex to the flummoxed Lucy, pretending to throw up. 'I've sold out,' he cries.

I had first heard *The Jacques Loussier Trio Plays Bach* during one of those musical Sunday mornings at home. On that album and many others, the French pianist used Johann

Sebastian Bach's compositions as the basis for jazz improvisations. I don't think I had ever really listened to the music of Bach before I heard these improvisations. But I was far from alone in my enchantment with Loussier: by the time of the Town Hall concert, his trio had sold millions of albums and been touring the world since before I was born.

Depending on your point of view, Loussier either practised the worst kind of musical miscegenation—playing a white man's jazz that bypassed the African roots of the genre via a long European detour—or he was a musical evangelist, spreading the love of improvisation and syncopated rhythm to millions of listeners who enjoyed it without knowing that improvising had been part of the music of ancient Greece, of Gregorian chant and medieval secular music, and a common and prized skill among European musicians for hundreds of years.

Today we know Johann Sebastian Bach as a prodigious composer, but in the first half of the eighteenth century he was regarded as an exceptional improviser. Beethoven, whose improvisations in performance were said to be more astounding than his printed compositions, wrote: 'Real improvisation comes only when we are unconcerned [with] what we play, so—if we want to improvise in the best, truest manner in public—we should give ourselves over freely to what comes to mind.'[23]

Until tonight's concert, Loussier's approach to Bach had been a mystery for my ears only, but now I watched it come to life. Even though I knew what *trio* meant, I could hardly believe that there were only three musicians on that wide stage. Somehow they created an entire world of sound. I can still see the double-bass player plucking the long strings of his instrument, one hand down low and the other up high at the neck, to produce those soft staccato steps that led to the opening of 'Pastorale in C Minor'.

Through my father's binoculars I saw the bassist and pianist communicating with their eyes: each lifting an eyebrow or nodding when it was time for the other to begin or finish their solo. The drummer shared a similar intimacy with the bassist, each smiling when some aspect of one's playing pleased the other. It surprised me to see how actively they listened, how attentive they were to each other's every note and gesture. They looked like good friends having the time of their lives. I wondered how they kept track of what they were playing and where they were in the piece. Loussier didn't refer to printed music although the bassist had some loose sheets of paper scattered near his feet. The drummer kept them all in time, but despite the responsibility he seemed so relaxed. I envied their familiarity with each other, their easy confidence on the stage, how they weren't embarrassed that everybody was looking at them.

I had played Dad's recording so many times that I recognised the Bach compositions, but the music came out differently on stage. How thrilling it was to hear the difference. The possibility that there could be such variation within the boundaries of a single piece thrilled me. I understood that the discrepancy between each performance of the same tune was intentional: the point was to honour the original composition with harmonically appropriate changes that became possible only within the notated boundaries of the melody and chords. My ears heard enormous freedom in music that offered flexibility within the larger context of an agreed form.

It surprised me to see the musicians sweating, or reaching for nearby glasses of water. These men had seemed like gods to me—that they felt sweaty and thirsty was liberating. It gave me hope that when I grew up I might be able to play like them. I wanted to play all of the instruments. I wanted to know how to sit at a piano with other people and produce the exquisite sensation that made it hard for me to sit still. I thought that to be a grown-up playing music like this on a stage for an audience was the greatest possible thing in the world to do. It didn't occur to me that these grown-ups were all men, or that this fact might be in any way significant.

When I handed back the binoculars, my father smiled at me with the pride of a man who knew his hard-earned money had not been wasted.

It wouldn't be easy. I would have to practise all the time, like Schroeder, to become good enough to play Bach. Then, when I could play Bach, maybe I could show him how much I loved his music by dancing with and around his beautiful melodies. How marvellous it would be to talk to a composer across time using my hands and my imagination at the piano, playing new variations on familiar themes. Schroeder might not have understood, but it was time for me to put away the toy piano. I needed to learn how to play Bach, so I could play like Jacques Loussier.

5

Alice May Morrison Taylor. It was hard to credit that my scary grandmother owned a maiden name of such glorious abundance. Until I saw her name written down in its entirety—at which time I was seized with the compulsion to read each word out loud, as if it were a poem—she had only ever been Granny, or, much later, the posthumous Alice Lloyd, with its three paltry syllables. But Alice May Morrison Taylor: the syllables, clustered in ones, twos and threes, had the gravitas of a complex chord played with two hands.

Alice was born on 8 July 1895, the second-oldest of five children born to Charlotte and James Taylor of 370 Dumbarton Road, Partick, in the west end of Glasgow. Home was one level in a three-storey tenement of sooty blonde sandstone, one of many rows of such housing built for the workers who had flooded into the city during the nineteenth century to work in its mills and shipyards. James Taylor worked for Denny's Shipyard, which sat at the mouth of the River Leven where it met the Clyde, just below Dumbarton Rock. Denny's was as famous as Charles Dickens.

The Taylors' firstborn, Anne, was named after her mother's mother, according to Scottish convention. But everyone knew her as Nance and the pretty one. In quick succession Alice gained three brothers—Vincent, Stephen and James—so that five children learned to squeeze into two bedrooms.

When I imagine how Alice recalled her childhood, I suspect it was the noise that first came to mind. Home was an incessant din of her brothers running after each other and yelling out until their mother's even louder rebukes quieted them. A constant scraping of chairs against cold stone and threadbare carpet, of knives and forks on chipped dinner plates, the heavy thud of her father's boots announcing the end of another long day's work.

In the year of Alice's birth, Glasgow was the fourth-largest port in Europe, and so important economically it was known as the second city of the British Empire. Positioned at the head of the Clyde, Glasgow conveniently faced the Americas, and the influence of that invisible shore rippled from the docks into every working-class home. By that time, shipbuilding had replaced the trade in cotton and tobacco, which had fuelled Glasgow's furnace for almost two hundred years. Shipbuilding companies flourished on the banks of the Clyde, and gradually the industry became the greatest in the world when Britannia ruled the waves. And the heartland of shipbuilding in Glasgow, which reached its peak just before World War I, was Partick. Between the censuses of 1881 and 1891, Partick's population rose more than 33 per cent from 27,396 to 36,538.[24]

On his certificate of marriage to Charlotte Speed on 3 March 1883, James Taylor's profession is listed as 'riveter and journeyman'. To be a journeyman meant that James had completed his apprenticeship and was employed by someone else, while riveting was one of those very specific, highly skilled trades that are both crucial and totally invisible. As with so many specialist occupations—air traffic controller, radiation oncologist, concert pianist—riveter didn't emerge as an apprenticed role until the technology developed that enabled and required it. Necessity may be invention's mother, but invention in turn can give birth to peculiar children; in the case of James's profession, the steel industry was the necessary precursor to the rise of specialist riveters.

The one photograph I have of Alice's father reveals a heavy-set man with a white handlebar moustache, wearing a grey wool suit with matching waistcoat, a beret and a bemused expression. I imagine James Taylor standing a few feet from the roaring cauldron where he works ten-hour days with his team driving blue-hot metal into pre-prepared holes in a sheet of steel. He's known these men since he was old enough to form memories. In and out of each other's houses along the streets they still live in, the same tenements his mother and father expired in when their shifts were through. The men are together at St Mary's Old Masonic Bar—a short walk along Dumbarton Road to number 165—and at Dowanhill Church, and here at the open mouth of the furnace, where the months have turned into years without their noticing. It's only sometimes, when he peels off his battered boots at the end of a long day and looks around at those familiar faces who depend on him, at the worn carpet and the tobacco-stained walls that feel sometimes as if they're closing in, or when one of his children is saying grace, that he's struck by how many years have floated away with the ships they've built.

Now James waits until the furnace operator determines the rivets are as hot as they can get; then, with one rivet glowing with pure heat on the end of his tongs, the operator throws it to his catcher man, standing by the joints that need riveting. The catcher pops the rivet into the hole and turns back to field the next one out of the oven, while James and his mate work together to set the rivet in place. One of them clasps its domed head in a purpose-built vice while the other hammers the unformed tail of the rivet so it mushrooms against the joint. In accordance with the second law of thermodynamics, the rivet is already beginning to cool, contracting against the joint. The force of pressure causing restriction, tightening; a metallic microcosm of the journeyman's life. James has inserted thousands of these things over the years to build the ships that float about the empire, but he still can't help but admire the unyielding perfection of a row of riveted joints.

The P&O passenger liner SS *Berrima*, on which Alice would eventually sail to the other side of the world, was one of about 370 Clydebuilt ships completed in 1913. The others were purpose-built for battle. The name *Clydebuilt* was synonymous not only with quality, but also with travel—whether for leisure or war.

There's no such thing as a riveter anymore, Rosie. These days steel rivets have been replaced by supremely strong bolts, and only two of those bustling Clydebuilt shipyards remain. The jagged polished chrome of the Glasgow Riverside Museum of Transport—designed by Zaha Hadid, no less—opened in 2011 on the site of a former shipyard. The shipwrights' labour has been commodified into a nostalgic tourist spectacle. The latest edition of the industry bible of specifications for steel construction includes no reference to steel rivets at all. In true 21st-century style, both the training and the tradesmen it took to install rivets in a single joint are redundant: instead of four skilled riveters, the new high-strength bolts require just two workers to install them.

As the shipping industry has gone the way of the British Empire, so Alice's high-street location has given over to conspicuous consumption. Today the entrance to 370 Dumbarton Road is squeezed between a Boots pharmacy and a Card Factory, one unassuming door in a long line of retail outlets in the tenements stretching along Dumbarton Road from Peel Street to Hamilton Crescent, which was renamed in 1931 as Fortrose Street. Being just across from the Merkland Street entrance to Partick train station, there's now a post office and a bank in the same block. If this were

Monopoly, the Taylors would have hit the jackpot with such a prime location—except that ownership was beyond their means. The Taylors' landlord was the one sitting on a small fortune. The most valuable object in their house was the family piano.

♫

The Taylors weren't the only ones on Dumbarton Road with a piano in their living room, though the instruments were still far from common in Partick parish. Reflecting the instrument's increasing accessibility to the lower rungs of the social ladder, piano sales grew much faster than the population. Between 1851 and 1910, piano production in Great Britain tripled from 25,000 to 75,000 units, while the population grew 66 per cent.[25]

How the Taylors came by their piano is lost to history, but probability suggests that they inherited it from a relative. Neither Charlotte nor James was musical, but they would have welcomed the gift and made room for it in their cramped home for the possibility of one of their children taking it up. Nance, as the older sister, would have had first dibs, though there was no money to pay for lessons. I picture Alice bringing the pale tip of her index finger to the surface of a yellowed key and looking along the keyboard, wondering what paths her fingers might travel once she knew how to play. I'm certain that as soon as she was old enough to know what the piano was, she wanted desperately to be able to play it. But as with everything else—her clothes, her chores, her side of the bed—time alone at the piano was something she would have to wait for until Nance tired of it.

To sit still and be able to touch the keys must have appealed to Alice on many levels. At the most practical level, playing the piano was the opposite of chores—it was a private world where there were no brothers, no jobs to do, no prettier sister to be compared to, no surveillance by Mother, or God. I like to imagine Alice sitting up as tall as she could make herself, her back straight and her arms relaxed. Did she dream of having lessons? Of playing for the church choir? She would need to wait until she was old enough to get a job so she could pay for a teacher.

6

'I BELIEVE YOU LIKE TO PLAY Buyeer, young lady,' said Mrs Wilcox. A few weeks earlier, on my seventh birthday, my parents had asked if I would like to learn to play a real piano. From my obsessive devotion to the toy version, they had concluded that mine was a love that would not burn fast and die.

Apart from my grandmother, my piano teacher was the oldest woman I had ever seen close up. Mrs Wilcox was tall and thin and walked with a slight stoop. She had a big round face that reminded me of an orange. She spoke with an English accent and looked me straight in the eye. I felt afraid of her, especially after she had suggested at my first lesson that Mum wait outside in the car.

'Buyeer?' I said, bewildered. I had never heard of him.

Mrs Wilcox grabbed one of her earlobes and rang it like a bell. 'By. Ear. Your mother told me you can play on your toy piano what you hear on records and the radio. Not everyone can do that, you know.'

At home, hunched over my instrument while nestled in the golden shag pile, sitting cross-legged in front of the turntable as if it were some high-fidelity altar, I played, paused and replayed individual tracks, picking my way across a few of the melodies Frank sang, such as 'Night and Day', 'I've Got You Under My Skin' and 'All of Me'. Away from the record player, I found that I had not only memorised the melodies but the lyrics too. But just because I could remember the words and copy the melody on my toy piano didn't mean I understood what Frank or Ella was singing about. What was a 'lush life'? And how could love be 'for sale'? It didn't disturb my parents that I listened to lyrics about adult relationships, no matter how coy the phrasing. In a general sense I knew that Frank sang about how men fall in love with women, but my concept of adult love, like my understanding of how his voice was contained in the grooves of the black vinyl disc I repeatedly spun, remained as remote and vague as the future.

No one quite knew for sure where Mr Wilcox was, or indeed if he had ever existed, but for decades Mrs Wilcox had taught piano and flute to Hunters Hill's schoolchildren from her home about halfway along the suburb's long, narrow peninsula. Her living room contained a sofa and two upholstered chairs, a cabinet full of books and knick-knacks, and her black upright piano. Through a large window one branch of a pale eucalyptus tree creaked in time to the invisible music of the breeze.

As Mrs Wilcox talked about the importance of listening carefully and sitting up straight and practising every day, I grew impatient. I didn't know what she was talking about, but I understood instinctively that if I remained still and was very polite, I might get to touch the piano in the corner. I couldn't take my eyes off it: the white keys looked as smooth and delicious as vanilla ice cream. And then there were the shiny surfaces of the black keys, and the piles of books and papers along its top. I had never been so close to a real piano before. The afternoon light skipped across the polished side closest to the window, reflecting the clouds and shadows.

'Would you like to come and sit at the piano?' Mrs Wilcox said at last, though it could only have been five or ten minutes.

Despite my eagerness to touch the keys, I approached the instrument with my hands by my sides, as if it were a horse that might flinch and run away. When I hopped up on the black leather piano stool, Mrs Wilcox helped me into what she called the *correct playing position.* My feet, encased in white socks with frilled edges and black patent Mary Janes, were still a year or so away from touching the floor. I saw my fingers hovering over the white notes as if it were the most natural thing in the world for them to do. The position felt slightly uncomfortable—my arms held aloft as they had been in my few dance classes—but somehow I already understood that in time the awkwardness would pass. Mrs Wilcox had the key to all the secrets the notes had to tell me, and one day soon I would know them.

♫

To practise on a piano between lessons, I had to walk from home around the corner and a short way up the steep incline of De Milhau Road to Mrs Weir's house. Mrs Weir and my mother were friends. I called her Mrs Weird, but not to her face. The journey, which took all of one minute, would today be considered too dangerous for a seven-year-old, with paedophiles allegedly lurking behind every tree.

My own fears were neatly internalised even if they were as obvious as daylight to the outside world. I clutched my beginner's book in front of my sausage-shaped torso and worried that Mrs Weir's son Andrew, who went to my school, would be home—I didn't want him to hear me fumbling around, trying to remember which note was which. He was a year older than me but did not play the piano. I couldn't understand how it was possible to have a piano in your living room and not at least try to play it. If I had a piano at home I knew I would play it every day.

When I arrived, Mrs Weird would have a biscuit and a glass of milk set on the kitchen table for me as if I were

Santa. The more she smiled the more embarrassing it was to make my first attempts to string notes together in front of her. I could hardly hear myself playing for worrying about what she thought. There was so much to take in, and I wanted to understand it all at once. While perfectionists understand that mistakes are inevitable, they prefer to make them in private.

One of my earliest tasks was to learn which note on the keyboard corresponded to the black circle with the long stalk on each of the first, second, third or fourth lines of the printed music. Mrs Wilcox had taught me the phrase Every Good Boy Deserves Fruit as a way to remember E-G-B-D-F, the name and order of the notes on the black lines in the right hand from low to high. The phrase stuck in my head but didn't help. I believed that good boys deserved chocolate or a new toy, but C's home wasn't on one of the lines. And there was no T for *toy*, in any case. The piano's alphabet was quite limited really, going only from A to G. With so few notes to learn, I suspected I'd have the instrument sorted out pretty quickly. The notes that sat in the white spaces between the black lines were easy to remember: F-A-C-E.

The quite ordinary Mrs Weird who had the piano was related to the Weirds who lived next door to us. But they really were strange, having an ant farm in their kitchen and driving to church every Sunday. The only ant my mother would tolerate in her kitchen was a dead ant; she depressed the bug-spray trigger on hapless insects with the zeal of a mass murderer. On Sundays, Dad was often gardening when the next-door Weirds drove past on their way to church; he'd stand up in his tattered white singlet and khaki work shorts and yell, 'Say one for me, Stella!' waving them off with his wood-handled garden shears.

My own experience of Sunday school had been short-lived. The photographic record suggests that I wore some great outfits to those Bible lessons. In remedial-sized handwriting we wrote down key points in the life of Jesus and recreated His most significant moments using coloured pencils in soft-cover booklets. Sunday school was where I'd heard stories about God switching on the lights on the first day, an old man who killed his son, a woman who ate an apple. But one day, when I'd answered the question 'Who is Jesus Christ?' with a triumphant 'A superstar!', the

Sunday school teacher had seen fit to call my mother. At this rate, it would take more than a pair of polished shoes and a purple dress to get me into heaven.

Ironically my debut performance at one of Mrs Wilcox's regular student concerts, after just three weeks of lessons, occurred in the church hall where I had incorrectly identified Jesus. As I strutted towards the piano, I did not imagine that 'Indian Dance' was a racial profile of indigenous Americans set to music or a simple tune requiring almost no dexterity. 'You should be able to keep a twenty-cent piece on the back of your hand without it falling off,' Mrs Wilcox had said at one of my first lessons. On stage, my left hand stayed in place for the one-minute duration, hopping up and down on two notes played by two fingers. While this was going on, the right hand pretty much stayed where it was, too, hovering over a five-note span and depressing the keys in a repeated pattern. The other thing that didn't move was my hair, which my mother had pulled back so tightly from my seven-year-old face that it made me look as though I was still only six.

Like Czerny's teaching method 137 years earlier, Mrs Wilson's assumed from her student's first lesson that the goal of playing the piano was performance. In this respect she also emulated Flaubert's Madame Bovary, who despaired of practising without the prospect of an audience: 'Why should she play? Who would hear her? Since she could never sit on a concert stage in a short-sleeved velvet gown, running her light, graceful fingers over the ivory keys of an Erard piano and feeling the ecstatic murmur of the audience flow around her like a warm breeze, there was no point in going through the boredom of practising.'

I wore cotton rather than velvet and sat at a Yamaha upright in a church hall rather than at a grand Erard on a concert stage, but the silent attention of an audience was intoxicating. There was no radio blaring out the news every half-hour, and my brother had no choice but to sit still and listen to me. He and Dad would catch up with the footy in the car on the way home. The piece was so simple that I felt confident performing it, and to play solo made me feel special, no matter how fledgling my talent. I smiled throughout my minute on stage, delighted at the way my hands worked accurately in the public spotlight, relieved to discover that I genuinely enjoyed playing for others, and excited about my next lesson and having new pieces to learn. There was no 'ecstatic murmur' among the audience as in Madame Bovary's fantasy, but the applause was genuine. Afterwards, over tea and biscuits up the back of the hall, I smiled at compliments from familiar faces.

Soon after the concert, Mrs Wilcox suggested to my mother that I would improve more quickly if I had my own instrument. Mum promptly informed my father that the time had come to buy me a real piano.

Her clairvoyant had been right.

With my father I roamed a piano display room, thrilled at the thought of my practice sessions at Mrs Weird's house coming to an end. Surrounding me were black pianos, brown pianos, and a vast gleaming piano the colour of white chocolate. Until that moment I hadn't realised that grand pianos came in different sizes, or that anyone other than Liberace had access to a white one. We proceeded past the

Steinways and the Bösendorfers, the Kawais and the Beales, to the display of modest uprights that occupied the far corner of the room. A salesman began to pay us attention using his peripheral vision.

Dad nudged me onto a stool. 'Go on, play something,' he said.

Neither of us had any idea what to look for in buying a piano. I was sitting before a small reddish-brown Yamaha, transfixed by the sheen of the wood and the polished white notes, smooth as the collars on the shirts Mum ironed for Dad. Did brand-new pianos arrive by plane, or by sea? How would you get one out of the store and into your house? And where would your mother allow you to put it? At seven I had no sense of what a piano cost, or what other purchases my parents had deferred so that I could have one.

Our generation-spanning ignorance must have been obvious to the salesman, who drew nearer as I attempted to reproduce by memory a simple melody from one of my beginner's books. In my nervousness, the fingers of my right hand tripped over each other.

'Oops! That's the wrong note,' I said, before playing the melody correctly.

'The important thing is she knew she'd made a mistake,' said the salesman, now standing at my father's elbow and confident of a sale.

Dad interpreted his ego-stroking comment as proof of my precocious talent, and the chestnut upright arrived at our house ten days later.

A shining Japanese-manufactured piano now stood in one corner of what in our house was known as the Sitting Quietly room. Before now I had only ever gone in there to read, curled up on a high-backed olive-green sofa chair. It was a great place to be by myself. Covered in pale golden wallpaper and straw-coloured shag pile, the room featured a square glass coffee table that only ever had one empty ceramic bowl sitting perfectly in its centre. A still-life painting, minus the life.

When I lifted the lid of the keyboard for the first time, I was surprised to see a sash of purple felt draped across it, as if the Yamaha had just won a beauty contest for its perfect but modest proportions. I didn't know which note to touch first. The black keys looked like the mane of a wild horse. I pressed a white key near the middle with the tip of my right index finger, as if I feared it would bite me. The instrument settled in the tufted carpet, its brass pedals hovering above it like three tiny feet. You could raise the top of the piano and prop it open with an in-built stick that stood up in a special cavity in the underside of the lid. When you played the piano with its lid open, it echoed and rumbled more loudly than when the lid was closed.

After a few days my mother placed one of her porcelain figurines along the piano's closed top. Her Lladró collection—polished tableaux of labour and romance that included a pair of courting Mexican peasants (complete with sombreros) and a captain of the British Navy consulting his map of territories yet to be colonised—abhorred a vacuum. She had often mentioned that she would have loved to learn the piano when she was a girl, but that her family was too poor to afford lessons. Now, with the upright making itself comfortable in the Sitting Quietly room of her own home, my mother chose to dust it as if it were the largest figurine in her collection, rather than touch the keys directly with her fingers. In later years I would remove the figurines so I could practise with the lid open, but back then I had to ask her to remove them. There was a connection between my mother's insistence that my hair be tied back at all times and her preference for keeping the lid of the piano closed, but I failed to see it then.

The piano tuner, who arrived two weeks after the instrument, wasn't happy about its location. Its back was exposed to the large window that looked east to the Tarban Creek bridge, where the sun rose on the cars and trucks that drove across it all day and night.

'He said, "You've got two walls of glass meeting in this corner. The sun will stream in and cause it to go out of tune,"' my mother reported when I got home from school. 'He said it's the worst place for the piano.' She shook her head, her eyes flashing at the memory. 'The hide of him, telling me where to put the piano!'

I felt sorry for the tuner. He probably knew what he was talking about, but not that it was no use offering a contrary opinion. The only alternative would have been to move the piano against the shortest wall and put the cream sofa in the sunny corner. Even I could see that this wouldn't work: the sofa was too big. Anyway, my mother was right—the sunlight would have faded the fabric.

'I told him that's too bad and that's where it's staying,' she said with the sharp edge in her voice that acted on me as a bridle did a horse. I was certain the piano tuner wouldn't have mistaken her tone either, before remembering he was self-employed and tuning the instrument where it stood.

♫

On Wednesdays I could hardly wait for school to end so I could sit on my teacher's smooth black leather piano stool and explore her books of music manuscript. Like many beginners, I had started with John Thompson's series, including the classic *Teaching Little Fingers to Play*, before moving on to Robert Schumann's *Album for the Young*, along with *The Children's Bach* by Johann Sebastian himself. I can still picture those creamy quarto-sized pages crammed with squiggles and lines and dots and white-faced notes and black blobs—and running through them all, like a comb through the knots in my hair, the five lines for each clef, treble and bass, right hand and left (more or less). 'I didn't understand anything until once I saw a musical staff at the top of a greeting card,' wrote Russian poet Marina Tsvetaeva of her struggle to learn notated music, 'where, instead of notes sitting on the staff, there were—sparrows! Then I understood that notes live on branches, each one on its own branch, and from there they jump onto the keys, each one onto its own. And then it makes a sound.'[26] In her 1934 essay 'Mother and Music', Tsvetaeva—who became one of the twentieth century's finest poets—confesses she disliked simultaneously reading and playing music, feeling that the notes hindered her. My experience was the opposite: to me the written notation was a puzzle or a secret that I could understand, if I paid attention to Mrs Wilcox and practised every day.

My mother had taught me to read letters and words, but learning to read music was my independent discovery. The very idea that a circle with a straight tail corresponded to a particular note, that a symbol written on paper indicated not only the precise pitch of a sound but its duration too, was so intoxicating I kept coming back to the piano stool for more. But reading music was exhausting—you needed to be able to read up and down, to the right and to the left, using your full concentration. And even when you did that, the music never meant anything more than the pretty sounds it made. The combination of dots and lines weren't like letters forming words; they weren't about anything. Still, I was learning to speak a new language, and I didn't want to stop talking. 'I know every thought in your head,' my mother sometimes said to me as a warning against discord; but she didn't know this. My anxiety to please her was countered by the pleasure I felt at the piano, my little fiefdom of discipline and delight. As the only one in my family who understood what the black notes and straight lines meant, I associated notated music with privacy and power, and the piano became a secret place I could go where no one else could follow.

As I progressed, getting the notes under my short impatient fingers was only one aspect of learning a new piece. Another was learning the vocabulary of music's written language, which was primarily Italian. The pages of my Bach *Two-Part Inventions*, a classic teaching text for beginners, were filled with Italian words and phrases. *Allegro tranquillo* at the top left of the two pages of 'Invention 13 in A minor', for example, instructs the pianist as to the speed (*allegro* means fast) and tone (*tranquillo*, no prizes for guessing) at which she should embark—and though I'd never had a problem with playing fast, the tranquil part was more elusive. *Presto* was my preferred tempo to play, though *andante*, for a walking speed, was my favourite adjective. I loathed *largo*; its slow pace required patience, restraint, and what Mrs Wilcox described as an *emotional connection with each note*, whatever that meant.

There was the fancy *f* that I knew meant *forte*, loudly, and the *mf* that added *mezzo* to the *forte* and indicated a volume about halfway between *f* and the *p* for playing softly, *piano*. There were the signs that looked like the bobby pins my mother used to keep my hair in place, which, depending on the way they opened, indicated I should gradually get either louder or softer. Beneath one bobby pin the instruction grew quite specific: *decresc. poco a poco*. How I loved that *poco a poco*: to get softer, little by little. The abbreviation *dimin.* told the pianist to become quieter—in English, to diminish it—while *cresc.* suggested it was time to play louder.

♫

In 1723, Johann Sebastian Bach described his fifteen two-part *Inventions* as exercises composed for 'amateurs of the keyboard, and especially the eager ones'.[27] He wrote them for his then nine-year-old son Wilhelm Friedemann. By 'keyboard' Bach referred to the harpsichord and clavichord (clavier), which the pianoforte would not dislodge for several decades. About 250 years later, when I was two years into my lessons—near Wilhelm Friedemann's age and learning Bach's 'Two-Part Invention number 13'—my twentieth-century edition marked gradations of *piano* and *forte*. The terms sum up the transformative difference of the instrument from those two earlier keyboards: it can play from soft to loud. Because of that development, in the late eighteenth century the pianoforte not only became the dominant keyboard instrument but also quickly made its predecessors redundant.

An invention is a short work for keyboard defined by its counterpoint. In the case of a two-part invention, two independent and different voices operate in harmony with each other. It was a model for any relationship, really, all those variations of rhythm and melody, all those patterns of the left-hand imitating or varying what the right hand had just played, squeezed into twenty-four bars (in the case of Invention 13) of independent development and harmonious empathy. Just as in Bach's more structurally complex *Preludes and Fugues*, the *Two-Part Inventions* feature the playful sharing of melody between the hands. As in a game of tennis, the right hand throws a fragment of melody after two bars to the left hand, which keeps it for two bars before lobbing the task of melodic development back into the right hand's court. Again the left hand answers a melodic scrap in the right, only for the conditions to be reversed later in the composition. And on it goes, back and forth across the net of staves and bar lines. A game between two hands, two voices, in which there is harmony and agreement; and if discord should arise, the musical clash soon resolves itself. More Björn Borg than John McEnroe.

During our lessons Mrs Wilcox hovered over my right shoulder holding her yellow pencil, worn down to a stub. In the Invention, in addition to helpfully inserting a numeral above an especially tricky note to indicate the best finger for me to use, she took her pencilled annotations one step further: she altered the left-hand notation in one bar so my nine-year-old hand could manage it. Even then I wondered what Johann Sebastian would have made of her editorial intervention.

The future novelist George Eliot was an eager amateur pianist from girlhood, when the world knew her as Mary Anne Evans. As an adult, she described in her letters how playing the piano gave her a 'fresh kind of muscular exercise as well as a nervous stimulus'.[28] As a writer, she endowed several of her female characters with musical talent. In *The Mill on the Floss*, Eliot channelled her passion for the instrument in the musical preferences of her heroine Maggie Tulliver: 'The mere concord of octaves was a delight to Maggie, and she would often take up a book of studies rather than any melody, that she might taste more keenly by abstraction the more primitive sensation of intervals.' If Maggie was managing octaves single-handedly, her handspan was broader than mine. It wasn't the remote musicianship of the virtuoso that captured Eliot's imagination; she understood the physical and intellectual challenges the instrument presented to its students, and empathised with her heroine's faults in playing. 'Hurrying the tempo . . . was certainly Maggie's weak point,' Eliot noted.

The beginner's temptation to hurry was hard to curb. In his instructional *Letters to a Young Lady*, Czerny warns against the common 'error of accelerating the time'.[29] The off-white pages of my first music books are covered in notes from two distinct hands. Mrs Wilcox's handwriting is long and slim like she was, neat from years of writing in the margins of music manuscripts at odd angles over the shoulders of her students. All her annotations remind me about tempo. In my own hand, rounder and thicker like my prepubescent torso, are my colloquial translations: *Slow down! Do NOT rush!!*

And then there were the punctuation marks, such as the dot beneath a note that told me to play it *staccato*—to jump off it—as opposed to the smooth evenness of the ideal *legato.* I had a lazy tendency when first learning a piece to ignore phrase marks, which comprise the internal punctuation of any composition: a musical phrase shapes a series of notes or measures of a piece with its own beginning, middle and end. And just as disrespect for punctuation, now epidemic in the age of instant-messaging, leads to misunderstandings and garbled communication, so my rushed delivery of melodies minus precise phrasing resulted in interpretations that for Mrs Wilcox were semiliterate at best.

Raising my eyes from Mrs Wilcox's keyboard, I was often shocked to see myself in the shining black surface of the piano. It wasn't the same as seeing my reflection in the mirror over my bedside table, where the ribbons my mother tied around my pigtails hung above a tiny vase of fresh flowers she sometimes placed there. Staring into the piano's black mirror was more like seeing into the future, recognising for the first time the possibility of another version of myself, glimpsing the girl I would become, the girl who could play the piano and understand the world around her through her fingertips, and let her hands speak for her when she could not.

7

At the piano, Alice May Morrison Taylor picked out the notes she saw in her mind's eye, repeating under her breath the new hymn the choir had sung this morning. When she listened to the choir she pictured the shape of what they sang. Didn't everyone? Sometimes the notes marched in a line as straight as Dumbarton Road. Other times the melody would soar as if to the top of Dumbarton Rock, then float back down to the Clyde. If Alice could keep its shape in her mind's eye during the service and the walk home, she knew she would be able to remember it when she returned to her piano. She had come to think of the piano as hers, because Nance had given up all pretence of playing it, and, despite the organist at church being a man, their parents and brothers considered playing the piano as something only girls did.

The Dowanhill United Free Church was ten minutes from home. On the way there, one of her brothers would crack the joke about how it should be downhill, like its name. Nance giggled every time, but it drove Alice to distraction. Her favourite moment was rounding the corner into Hyndland Street and seeing the steeple pointing straight up to God. Soon she would be inside the church and singing, even if she were sandwiched in a pew between her fidgeting brothers instead of up the front with the choir where she just knew she belonged.

'Surely there are quicker ways, Mother,' James Taylor grumbled as they walked home along Hyndland Street toward Dumbarton Road.

'It's half a mile whichever way we go,' his wife replied. 'When Alice joins the choir she'll have to get there and back by herself, and you know very well this is the simplest.'

Every Sunday Alice watched the conductor, old Mr Cunningham, her eyes glued to his narrow shoulders as he moved his arms in front of the choir, trying to imagine exactly what he was doing. As long as she could remember, she had yearned to join the choir.

But musically speaking, Dowanhill United was a serious business: membership of the choir was by invitation only.

'Mr Cunningham told me today he'd be happy to have you join the choir when you turn twelve,' her mother had said the previous Sunday afternoon, unpegging the dry sheets from their section of the common clothesline. Alice had bent to help her fold them, trying to contain her excitement. 'It's God's gift to you, your voice,' her mother had said, the peg lodged in one corner of her mouth keeping her tone flat. 'Sure as eggs you didn't get it from us.'

Despite the peg, Alice had heard the quiet pride in her mother's voice. But twelve? She had only just turned eleven. How could she possibly wait that long?

8

THE PIANO STOOL QUICKLY BECAME THE most comfortable seat for me in any house. At home I was rolled out at dinner parties to entertain my parents' friends, and on Christmas Day post-pudding for members of my extended family who preferred Bacharach to Bach but politely clapped anyway.

Because I was a strong sight-reader—meaning that I could play credibly through a piece that was new to me—by the age of ten I was a regular accompanist to the violinists, singers and flautists of my neighbourhood. Like those of any freelancer, my gigs came through my immediate network and word-of-mouth recommendations. Mrs Wilcox's strongest flute students—which I also became, for a time—needed accompanying at her regular concerts, where I was now a featured soloist at the end of the program. While I rose to the challenge of solo performances, increasing anxiety over forgetting the notes or making an obvious mistake had begun to cloud my enjoyment. I found myself gravitating toward the variety, novelty and companionship of the accompanist's job: to help the soloist sound their best. A budding violinist at primary school asked me to perform with her for a church concert; a local singer needed me to help her rehearse for an upcoming audition. I said yes to everyone. Accompanying wasn't about me—it was about making the other musician feel secure.

Sight-reading is the process of converting musical information from visual signs and symbols into sound. It's a feat of short-term memory built on the solid ground of cultural familiarity with the type of music set before the musician: a combination of nature and nurture. Research has shown that proficient sight-readers look further ahead in the music than their less fluent counterparts, managing to process and remember a larger eye–hand span—the gap between reading the notes and actually playing them—than other musicians. Similar to reading language by expectation (the unfortunately named 'chunking'), the effective sight-reader recognises patterns of notes as a single unit.

Sight-reading is an addictive business, because by definition a musician requires vast amounts of fresh notation to develop the skill in the first place, and subsequently to satisfy the need for more music. French philosopher Roland Barthes, a highly proficient sight-reader, has been described as 'insatiable' for new music.[30] I know this particular lust. I understood musical promiscuity long before any other, always looking for the next piece to play, whether alone or with others. In my case the talent for sight-reading led me to accompanying, which in turn made me a stronger sight-reader, but this isn't an inevitable path. Barthes sought only new pieces for solo piano, which he would perform every morning for an audience of one—his mother.

♫

Looking back, I can see there was little coincidence that I practised every day before dinner, when invariably my mother would be preparing the meal in the kitchen—right beside the Sitting Quietly room. It was crucial to me that my mother heard me as I played. Sitting at my piano and not being able to see her through the dividing wall, I associated the tones of her voice with the pitch and rhythm of musical notes. Though her words didn't correspond precisely to any single note, their patterns translated easily enough: in the case of *ve-ry good*, into two quavers and a crotchet, with an emphasis on the rising pitch of the second word; in the case of *that's nice, darling*, four quavers in a symmetrical u-shape that fell from and ascended to the same pitch. In this way my mother's rising and falling intonation became the essential accompaniment to my domestic piano performances.

Because I was as sensitive to the nuances of my mother's voice as a seismograph to an earthquake, the worst possible sound was her silence.

One day I helped her fold invitations to the local Rotary Club art show, an enormous act of unpaid labour that my father undertook each year like a volunteer Sisyphus. Usually Mum and I chatted or sat in a companionable quiet, but as the afternoon wore on a cloud came over the silence.

I don't know how I knew my mother's mood had changed; I could just sense that she was upset about something despite showing no outward sign of it.

I pointed to the pile of sealed invitations in the centre of the kitchen table where we worked. By now there were hundreds of them. 'Look, Mummy,' I ventured to puncture the quiet, 'there's a wall between us.'

'There certainly is, my girl,' she said sharply, as the temperature around the table plummeted. 'There certainly is.' She continued to fold invitations while her face froze into the stony silence that could last for days. Talk about a lesson in metaphor.

Her tone sliced me to my stomach, but already I knew better than to ask if anything was the matter. Nothing ever was.

Years later, I wondered if she felt excluded by my relationship with my father, which was bound up in our love of music. It makes me sad to think that she might have longed for the two of us to share something of our own, and perhaps felt—despite the hours we spent together reading and talking—that we did not. So calling out to her from my piano stool wasn't for coaching or technical improvement: it was for reassurance that she remained pleased. It was she for whom I played, her approval that I sought. The need to hear my mother's brief encouragements was insatiable. Our ritual of call and response provided regular confirmation that everything was still all right.

♫

I am grateful to my mother for teaching me to keep my ears open at all times for nuance and imminent catastrophe. I developed a finely honed sixth sense for when a musician needs reassurance about when precisely to come in again after several measures of rest, or a subtle advance sounding of the note she is due to sing. Which phrases need extra punctuation, or where in the score the soloist is likely to start running ahead of the tempo. My capacity for attentive listening, when paired with the sight-reading, made me a popular accompanist.

Away from the piano, I was less charismatic. At Hunters Hill Public School, Greta Mitchell wielded social power over me like my mother did in every other aspect of my life. Recently Greta had excommunicated me from her circle without warning. Somehow she had the authority to decide who was in and who was out, as if by being in the same group of friends we formed a scale whose notes only she knew. I was devastated: I looked up to Greta, who had olive skin and played the cello. But she no longer wanted to make even the slightest eye contact with me. When my mother sometimes stopped talking to me or pointedly refused eye contact, I knew, deep down, that her silent withdrawal—those hours and days that felt as if they lasted for weeks—would end eventually. She never explained her silences, though I understood that I had done something wrong. Greta didn't explain herself, either, but her decision was final. At home I cried at the piano and sobbed into Gail's matted hair.

'What a lot of rot!' my mother exploded when I explained through tears what had happened. 'Why do you want Greta to be your friend, for god's sake? Get yourself some new friends.' The concision and force of her blast stunned me as if I had been wounded. She turned back to the kitchen sink, where potatoes awaited peeling.

What more was there to say, even if I could have found my voice? Empathy was in short supply around our house, whether you were a permanent resident or, like the piano tuner, just visiting. Clearly, the things I felt or had trouble explaining weren't for telling other people but for keeping to myself. I'd learned my lesson, and I'd never share anything important with my mother again. 'To feel anything strongly was to create an abyss between oneself and others who feel strongly perhaps but differently,' Virginia Woolf's heroine Rachel Vinrace concludes in *The Voyage Out*. 'It was far better to play the piano and forget all the rest.' Like Rachel, I stayed quiet except at the piano, where my fingers spoke with increasing confidence and fluency.

♫

Behind most talented girls at the piano is a highly influential mother. Maria, the mother of Marina Tsvetaeva, was a gifted amateur pianist. But Maria's father refused her ambition to pursue a professional music career, objecting to the idea of women performing in public. In this attitude Mr Tsvetaeva agreed with most people of the Victorian era, who regarded the stage as next door but one to the brothel. In Miles Franklin's 1901 novel *My Brilliant Career*, on learning that Sybylla Melvyn entertains notions of taking singing instruction and 'going on the stage', her grandmother says insistently: 'promise me you will never be a bold, bad actress'.

In 'Mother and Music', Marina Tsvetaeva writes about how her mother transferred her professional goal to her daughters. Marina wasn't the boy whom her mother expected to deliver in 1892. From the moment of her birth, she became her mother's plan B: 'When, instead of the longed-for, predetermined, almost preordained son Alexander, all that was born was just me, mother, proudly choking back a sigh said: "At least she'll be a musician."'

Poor Marina. At least my mother's psychic had been able to confirm my gender and musical tendencies prior to my birth. Great expectations are best managed in advance. Marina's thwarted mother told her: 'My daughters will be the "free artists" I wanted so much to be.' And then she forced Marina, the one daughter who showed some natural aptitude for music, to practise for hours daily from the age of four.

'You'll sit through your two hours—and like it!' Marina reports Maria saying to her in the tone other mothers might reserve for the eating of vegetables. Nothing is free, least of all freedom.

In 1906 Marina was headed straight for the Moscow Conservatory when her mother died of tuberculosis. The budding poet-pianist was fourteen. 'I certainly would have finished at the Conservatory and emerged a fine pianist,' she reflected almost thirty years later, 'for the essential capacities were there.' Instead she became a writer and composed 'Mother and Music' as a prose tribute to the fierce ambivalence of the love between mother and daughter. 'After a mother like that I had only one alternative: to become a poet,' she writes.

Maria's high ambition for her daughter to become a concert pianist is radically different from the common expectations of women pianists held throughout the nineteenth century, when it was believed they should be competent but not too good. This attitude is prevalent in Jane Austen's novels, in which remarkable skill at the piano is something not to be remarked. In *Emma* (1815), Jane Fairfax's extreme skill as a pianist places her in a morally shady corner of Austen's world; the characters loved hearing Miss Fairfax play, but their author was dubious about the real value of such ability. Despite Jane's talent and beauty, she is never a threat to Emma as the heroine of the story because of her secretive relationship with Frank Churchill, the donor of the sumptuous piano whose provenance remains a mystery for most of the novel.

In *Pride and Prejudice* (1813), Mary is the most musically accomplished Bennet sister, but Austen has little patience with her: 'Mary had neither genius nor taste; and though vanity had given her application, it had given her likewise a pedantic air and conceited manner, which would have injured a higher degree of excellence than she had reached.' She prefers the heroine, Elizabeth, who 'had been listened to with much more pleasure, though not playing half so well.'

The most famous virtuosa of the nineteenth century was Clara Wieck, known as Clara Schumann after her marriage in 1840 to the composer Robert Schumann. Clara's father, the pedagogue Frederick Wieck, had groomed her from the age of five for a career as a concert pianist. Despite a long and influential career as a performer, she encouraged her daughters Marie and Eugenie to teach rather than become soloists. They worked alongside her as teaching assistants at Hoch Conservatory in Frankfurt in the 1880s, helping students not yet at the technical level to study directly with Clara.[31] The majority of those wishing to study with the mother had no choice but to study first with one of the daughters—an impressive feminist twist on the Biblical promise of the Son being the only way to the Father.

As an aspiring pianist, Australian author Ethel Florence Lindesay Richardson—better known by her pseudonym, Henry Handel Richardson—sailed with her mother via the Cape of Good Hope to the Leipzig Conservatorium in 1888. In Leipzig, Richardson's loyalty to the piano was tested by her love of literature. It was Tolstoy whom she propped on her music stand to read while she 'ploughed through the needful but soul-deadening scales and exercises'. In her 1948 autobiography, *Myself When Young*, Richardson writes of not wanting to disappoint her mother:

> Here was I, who had been brought to Leipzig at what, for Mother, represented a considerable outlay; on whose behalf she put up with living abroad, which she detested, among people she didn't like and whose language she could not master. Yet all this she was willing to endure, provided she might take me back to Australia a finished pianist, there to make not only money but a name for myself.[32]

A professional pianist, making her living in the country in which she had been born and raised: that was all her mother asked. But she had fallen in love—in Germany, with a penniless intellectual to boot. 'For me now to blurt out that I didn't propose to put my training to any use, but, instead, contemplated marrying an insignificant young man, would be a cruel blow to her dreams and ambitions.'[33] Like Marina Tsvetaeva, Henry Handel Richardson didn't become a professional musician or put her studies directly to use; but the love of music travels along winding pathways, and in her case produced fiction in which the piano figured prominently. In her 1908 debut novel, *Maurice Guest*, she describes the tragedy of a young pianist who arrived in Leipzig in the 1890s, wanting desperately to be a concert artist, only to embark on a self-destructive and ruinous relationship with another musician.

Tsvetaeva's understanding that she would be a poet, not a musician, came as a relief. Yet it was her relationship with her mother, forged at the piano, that shaped her poetry. Her writing was inextricably linked with music because her mind had been shaped by her mother's passion for it. The torrent that flowed from her pen over the next thirty years reflected a sensibility that had been immersed in a 'pianohood' which replaced her childhood. Reflecting on the hours she spent at the instrument as a child, Tsvetaeva saw that it gave her, as an aspiring poet, a place that was both part of her and apart from her. A way of seeing one thing through another: a double vision in which she could be inside and outside her experience at the same time. To play the piano was a simultaneous act of self-discovery and self-expression, a powerful act of metaphor.

I can only be eternally grateful that neither my mother nor father played the piano, and that they outsourced my instruction to Mrs Wilcox. When I first started learning to play, I was so eager to improve that I sat at the piano daily. Other parents had to force their children onto the piano stool or bribe them with television or ice cream. My parents, who were thrilled simply to be able to afford lessons for their daughter, never applied any pressure on me to practise. I applied more than enough of my own. There was so much internalised pressure that it felt as if there was no pressure at all, because it was there all the time. I rode the tension like a monocycle and never fell off.

9

At the front gate of my new high school, I arrived early and staked out a position like a guard dog expecting its master. In my pleated grey hound's-tooth tunic, my action-back creases ironed to perfection, I waited for my friend Suzanne. As the one girl out of six hundred whom I knew, she had agreed to meet me at the gate and show me around. Thanks to sitting straight-backed at the piano as I practised my scales and arpeggios every day, I stood erect in what I believed was the image of grown-up poise. My dark brown hair was gathered in a thick ponytail—as per the school's commandment that loose hair must not touch the collar—and tied with a ribbon whose shade of navy was also stipulated. I scrutinised every passing anonymous face, the tide of anxiety rising in my chest. Little women scurried towards their classrooms like they were boarding Noah's Ark. Pairs of eager eyes, tightly braided pigtails and polished black shoes stamped up the lane two by two. In this environment, survival clearly depended on having a partner. But for a long time I failed to grasp this life lesson. Years later I would be struck with a strong sense of déjà vu while shopping alone at Ikea.

My mother was much more excited about my first day at Wenona than I. She had set her heart on my attending the school ever since she'd first admired its pale grey uniform, worn by the girls who rode the bus she took home from her weekly shopping trip to David Jones in Sydney's central business district. A keen observer of the surfaces of things, she took in the ribbons trailing from tidy ponytails, the shiny Clarks shoes, and the neat rows of metal braces on rebellious teeth. In a singular act of synecdoche, she took the part for the whole and concluded that the school would make a suitable environment for her musical daughter. Neither she nor my father had any information on Wenona's intellectual credentials. They had conducted no investigation into the quality of its musical training. And they had spared little thought to the daily commute required to get me there and back for the six years they planned on paying for me to study there. As it turned out, depending on the precise combination of bus, ferry and train, my round trip took between two and three hours every day. One morning in my final year, squeezed into a crowded bus farting its way up the hill to the school, I calculated that I had spent about five months of my life on public transport. But, as always, I said nothing. I had learned how important it was to keep all my surfaces polished and shining. My wayward front teeth were the only visibly defiant thing about me.

At some point a senior girl approached me as I waited for Suzanne. She saw my erect posture for the rigid terror that it was. She must have been seventeen, but to me she seemed a giant of a woman who contained bodies of knowledge—let alone knowledge of bodies—far beyond my powers of cognition. Smiling gently, she asked if I needed any help. I shook my head, willed threatening tears to subside, and advised in my best polite voice that I was waiting for a friend, thank you. She hovered briefly then retreated. I was seized by the fear that Suzanne had walked straight past me in that crucial lost minute. Unbeknown to me, most girls arrived via the rear gate at the opposite side of the school. I turned my head back to the front entrance, waiting for a footstep that never came.

♫

'The piano is such a lonely instrument,' thinks Athena in Helen Garner's *The Children's Bach*, 'always by yourself with your back to the world.' My experience during high school was the complete reverse: the only place I never felt lonely was at the piano. Accompanying the school assemblies two mornings every week for six years, I didn't care that all I got to play were Anglican hymns for hundreds of teenage girls in grey hound'stooth, because it was often a relief to be able to turn my back on them. Alone, most definitely; but never lonely.

Fifteen minutes into assembly in the school hall, just as hundreds of adolescent bottoms were starting to itch from sitting still on plastic seats, our headmistress Miss Jackson would look down from her podium on the stage to where I perched on the puckered black leather stool. In front of me was the Steinway, a majestic black grand on three bronze caster wheels. Its dark sheen threw the countless scratches of its lid and curved sides into high relief. My feelings were similar to those of Beth March in *Little Women*, who, when finally granted access to a grand piano, 'at last touched the great instrument, and straightway forgot her fear, herself, and everything else but the unspeakable delight which the music gave her, for it was like the voice of a beloved friend'. As slow and deliberate in her movements as a container ship, Miss Jackson would raise her imperious eyebrows above the rim of her large-framed glasses and nod gravely. By now I had my timing down to a fine art. At the moment I spied the tip of her silver bun dawning over the horizon of her forehead, I began, for the umpteenth time, the four-bar introduction to 'Jerusalem'.

And did those feet in ancient time

Walk upon England's mountains green:
And was the holy Lamb of God,
On England's pleasant pastures seen!

And did the Countenance Divine,

Shine forth upon our clouded hills?
And was Jerusalem builded here,
Among these dark Satanic Mills?

These lyrics, taken from William Blake's 1808 poem, suggest England might have briefly enjoyed a stint as heaven on earth if, as the apocryphal story has it, the young Jesus took a holy detour to Glastonbury in the company of his uncle Joseph of Arimathea. Somehow he'd turned up a few centuries early for the music festival. Performing the anthem was a dissociative exercise in separating the affecting melody and its melancholy harmonies from the ludicrous words—in my mind, the obvious answer to each of Blake's four questions as they were sung was a resounding no, no, no and no. The idea remained as fantastic as it had been in 1916 when

Sir Hubert Parry set Blake's poetry to music during wartime and turned 'Jerusalem' into a rousing nationalistic anthem.

'Thank you, Victoria,' said Miss Jackson, immune to my silent scepticism. As far as she was concerned, my name was Victoria and 'Jerusalem' was top of the hymnal pops. The idealised England in the anthem must have stirred our Lancashire-born leader, though it was no more likely that Jesus of Nazareth had blond hair and blue eyes than that he ever set foot in that faraway country. She fantasised about the grass being greener in a land quite literally more verdant than in her adopted home. One thing I knew for certain: Jerusalem was not to be found at the top of Walker Street, North Sydney.

Among the parents of the Kates and Sarahs and Fionas who populated my year, my father seemed to be the only one who performed anything close to physical labour outside of the home. As far as I could tell, other girls' fathers paid for their white-collared uniforms by working white-collar jobs. They were CEOs and lawyers and doctors and pharmacists, men who wore jackets and ties in office buildings. My father rose each day at dawn; put on his white singlet, khaki work shorts, long white cotton socks and boots; ate his cornflakes with warm milk; then drove his yellow Holden ute for miles to building sites where he worked alongside the men who subcontracted to him until the light gave out. My father was most proud of the fact that he had always been, from the time he was a teenager, his own boss. As a boy he was never interested in books or sitting still; he wanted to be out with his father on the farm, playing with his dog Barney, or pitching cricket balls at a water tank for batting practice. He laughs recalling how intimidated he was by the three girls in his class of seven students, who weren't only much smarter than he, but also the daughters of his teacher.

When my father finally had money to spend, he wasn't interested in strolling the Champs-Élysées or sailing Sydney Harbour in his own catamaran. He would provide for his family, whether or not they wanted him to. He would insist that his wife stop working outside the home though she loved her job as a comptometer operator—the precursor to the electronic calculator—at Amalgamated Wireless. He would send his children to expensive schools to have the formal education he did not. At his wife's urging, he would buy his daughter a piano.

It was just over one hundred years since the farmer Gabriel Oak first proposed to Bathsheba Everdene in Thomas Hardy's *Far from the Madding Crowd*. Oak sweetens his futile offer to make Bathsheba happy with the promise of her own instrument: 'You shall have a piano in a year or two—farmers' wives are getting to have pianos now—and I'll practise up the flute right well to play with you in the evenings.' By the late nineteenth century the piano might have been within reach of working-class families, and domestic music-making a common entertainment, but ownership of an instrument was hardly a sign of leisure. A farmer might be able to afford a piano, but not the time for his wife to play it. Anyway, Bathsheba wasn't having a bar of it.

A century later, the builder's wife had the time to play, but no longer the inclination. Their daughter would be the beneficiary of piano lessons. She would have a piano. She would be their instrument. 'The human soul needs actual beauty even more than bread,' D.H. Lawrence wrote in his 1929 essay 'Nottingham and the Mining Countryside'.

'The middle classes jeer at the colliers for buying pianos—but what is the piano, often as not, but a blind reaching out for beauty.'[34]

♫

'I think it's time you started competing in eisteddfods,' my new piano teacher announced to the middle of my back after a few weeks of lessons.

Mr McFarlane taught in a ground-floor studio apartment on the corner of two leafy streets in Sydney's lower north shore. Upstairs lived his mother, whom in eight years of instruction I never met but who made her presence felt, rattling pans and dragging chairs above my head like some irritable landlord of ancient mythology. The small teaching studio undulated in mounds of books and sheet music, as if a blizzard had never managed to melt. A bust of Beethoven frowned at me from the lid of the black upright piano, which was graffitied with scratches and fingerprints.

Mrs Wilcox had ambushed me at the end of my last lesson of the school year. 'There's nothing more I can teach you, dear,' she said by way of explaining that our lessons, like primary school, had come to an end. Though my feet now touched the floor, I was devastated. While I was proud of my technical accomplishments, after hurdling the annual grade examinations like a prize show pony, the news stung. I was not quite twelve. 'Mr McFarlane is his name,' she said, thrusting an envelope into my hand as I sat dumbstruck on her piano stool. 'Give that note to your mother. I've sent a few of my students to him over the years. You'll have to audition, but you'll get in. He's very good.'

E-sted-what?

Despite having been accepted as his student, I felt daunted by Mr McFarlane's thick glasses, his balding head of honey-coloured curls, and his severe demeanour. Even now I can't specify what I was so frightened of. I can't imagine anything in particular that caused my anxiety, because generally speaking, everything did: saying the wrong thing, playing the wrong note, it was all the same. I spent each piano lesson in a straitjacket of fear, looking directly ahead of me at Beethoven from the first greeting to the last minute, except when I cast furtive glances over my right shoulder now and then to gauge Mr McFarlane's speaking tone. Always on high alert for the nuances of my mother's voice, I wrongly heard in any voice of authority a punitive tone—and lived with the constant feeling that I had either just made a mistake or was about to.

My teacher sat a few feet behind me on a wooden chair, the ankle of one chubby leg resting on the knee of the other. He couldn't have been far into his thirties but he had a paunch that hid the waistband of his pants. Maybe one of the many things I feared was ending up as a piano teacher.

And had he said *compete*? I loathed any kind of competition. The word was shorthand for hours wasted on redundant activities such as field hockey, long jump and tunnel ball, not to mention the cacophony of the annual swimming carnival. How I loathed the swimming carnival, having to fake enthusiasm over human bodies moving through water. The stink of chlorine. The snap of elastic. It would be at least 11 p.m., after piano practice and homework, before I could return to my bed and the sensuous miseries of Tess d'Urberville.

'Eisteddfods are annual music competitions, arranged by age,' Mr McFarlane explained. 'You could still enter the twelve and unders this year, but I think you should compete in the fifteen and unders.'

It wasn't a question or open for debate. Part of me felt excited that my new teacher wanted to nudge me into the older age group where he thought I was the right technical fit, but after quickly jumping over the successive hurdles of new teacher, new school and new friends, I just felt like another rug was being pulled from my feet. What excited me was learning new music and becoming a better pianist; I thought I could achieve that by practising alone at home. Unlike my teacher, I failed to understand the role of competition in pushing a young pianist beyond the level that was comfortable for her.

Each time Mr McFarlane shifted in his seat I got a whiff of his body odour. A sleeveless white cotton singlet beneath his short-sleeved white polyester shirt did little to control his tendency to perspire, evinced by damp patches around his armpits. At moments like these I was grateful for the flute lessons I had taken with Mrs Wilcox. Despite a few years of diligent practice, the instrument had bored me rigid; on the subject of woodwinds, I sided with Oscar Wilde, who is attributed with describing the clarinet as 'an ill woodwind that nobody blew any good'.[35] The silver lining was that, having learned how to breathe using my diaphragm, I could hold my breath for a long time. Until I met Mr McFarlane, that skill had come in handy only when swimming underwater—an activity that never made it onto the swimming carnival program.

♫

'I practise every day as much as I can—I wish it were more for his sake,' wrote the twenty-year-old Jane Austen to her beloved sister Cassandra in September 1796. The man she refers to is her piano teacher, George William Chard, who had been the assistant organist at Winchester Cathedral since 1787.[36] Austen's father knew Chard, who was ten years older than Jane and by all accounts a lively and handsome man. To supplement his salary, Chard gave private lessons around Hampshire, riding forty miles to the rectory at Steventon to give lessons to Austen. She was his student during the time she started writing a novel with the working title *First Impressions*.

In a memoir, her niece Caroline Austen recalls that 'Aunt Jane began her day with music—for which I conclude she had a natural taste; as she thus kept it up—tho' she had no one to teach; was never induced (as I have heard) to play in company; and none of her family cared much for it.' Not a terribly inspiring environment to play in—closer to Mary Bennett than Jane Fairfax. Of Anne Elliot in *Persuasion* Austen wrote that 'in music she had been always used to feel alone in the world'. I wonder where she got that idea.

On leaving her childhood home in 1801, Austen sold her piano for eight guineas. She wrote little during the following years when she lived in Bath and Southampton; whether coincidence or not, neither did she have an instrument of her own. But in July 1809 she moved to Chawton, in Hampshire, where she had an allowance from her father's estate of twenty guineas per year, and few social obligations.

There's some confusion as to what proportion of her income went on her new piano. One source suggests that she blew a year and a half's allowance on it: thirty guineas on a twenty-guinea budget. Perhaps her wealthy brother Edward contributed. A second source suggests that by the time Austen moved to Chawton, her allowance was closer to fifty pounds a year. Even then, to spend thirty guineas on an instrument takes a giant bite from the budget.

However she paid for it, Austen's new piano announced to her family, and to herself, that at Chawton she would spend her money as she would spend her time: in writing books and playing the piano. Her domestic husbandry wouldn't be focused on the procurement of a husband—she was thirty-three and well beyond the likelihood of marriage. Neither she nor her piano would be moving from Chawton.

Today any Janeite can visit Chawton Cottage and inspect the author's music library. According to Caroline, Aunt Jane transcribed pages of waltzes and marches 'so neatly and correctly, that it was as easy to read as print'. One book in her own hand contains thirty-six songs complete with lyrics and keyboard accompaniment; another one mixing songs with instrumental works runs to eighty-four pages of manuscript. This can only be described as a manual labour of love. Anyone who has written out music by hand can attest to its being a job for only the most detail-oriented and fastidious copyist.

After ten years in which she wrote almost nothing, the arrival of Jane Austen's piano ushered in a period of great creativity. She began work on *Mansfield Park* in early 1811, revised *First Impressions* (which was later published as *Pride and Prejudice*), and in 1814 began writing *Emma*.

Austen's women pianists—Anne Elliott, Marianne Dashwood, Mary Bennett, Jane Fairfax—are products of their era: they dutifully play for others when requested, but do not actively seek opportunities to perform. To compete for a judge's approval or a vulgar trophy—that's the last thing an Austen heroine would do.

♫

To the untrained eye, the daunting number of notes in Bach's Prelude 2 in C Minor from the *Well-Tempered Clavier* give the appearance of ants crawling over the page. On closer inspection, the ants run rather than crawl, moving allegro almost from beginning to end. They're well trained, too, running in consistent semiquaver patterns that give every finger work to do. The trick to performing the prelude is to have perfect fingering—so that you never get caught midway through without the best possible finger to play a particular note—and to make sure you don't start off too quickly. If you begin too fast, then there's little room for acceleration during the six-bar section towards the end that Bach, with uncharacteristic prescriptiveness, indicated should be played presto.

Of course, nervous tension causes many amateurs to do the opposite, and I was no exception. Particularly in competitions such as the one I was performing in right now, inside a nondescript church hall somewhere on the northern beaches of Sydney. A location where almost every other girl my age was tanning her smooth shaved legs or frolicking in the surf on this hot Saturday afternoon.

But after so much practice, speed didn't worry me. My main concern was forgetting the notes. Though I had a knack for committing pieces to memory, I spent every solo performance in a bind of conflicting messages from my brain that assured me I wouldn't forget while at the same time instilling dread at the imminent likelihood of forgetting. I visualised the work in my mind's eye as my hands scurried over the keyboard, terrified and relieved at every turn.

The biggest threat was to stumble over the fingering, which would interrupt the largely unconscious flow of notes. Hardly any of the countless bits of information committed to memory—not just the notes, but also the structure of the piece, the tempo, the dynamics of how loud and how soft to play at any given moment; when to pause slightly, and when to accelerate just a touch; when to lift my right hand off the keyboard at the end of a phrase; when to depress the sustain pedal that ran a sequence of notes into one another; when to walk smoothly along the notes, legato, or to leap off each one in staccato fashion; and the fingering required, tucking the thumb underneath the index finger here, using the fourth rather than fifth finger there, so as to manage that jump in the next bar—occurred to me consciously while I played a piece from memory. The purpose of memorising is that, ideally, you're so thoroughly knowledgeable of the composition's mechanics that you can let your subconscious take them over while you concentrate on the emotional interpretation. To me, getting through a performance without a technical hitch—like the Olympic gymnast who stays upright when she lands that final flip—was the ultimate achievement. It was proof that somehow through intense repetitive practice the music had lifted off the page, flown like Tsvetaeva's sparrows into the air I breathed, and entered my bloodstream.

Clara Schumann was one of the first virtuosi to perform from memory in public. She had learned to memorise music from an early age, studying with her exacting father. Playing without printed music was sufficiently unusual that when she did so in an 1828 public concert at the age of nine, reviewers commented on the practice—and not favourably.[37]

Years of publicly performing don't abate your nerves at the prospect of your memory failing. Decades into her career as a concert artist, Clara confessed to a close friend, the composer Johannes Brahms, her increasing anxiety about performing without music: 'Though I am often so nervous from one piece to the next,' she wrote, 'I cannot make the decision to play from the music; it always seems to me that it is almost as though my wings were clipped.'[38] Clara had long been her father's caged bird. Wieck had trimmed those wings well; she didn't resort to having the music in front of her, but neither did she forget the notes.

For better and worse, Clara Schumann established the model for the concert instrumental virtuoso—and even for pianists in their earliest years of study—that continues to this day. My father couldn't have cared less if I played Bach with the music or 'by heart', as we used to say. But by virtue of the generations of solo instrumentalists who followed Clara's example, Mrs Wilcox and now Mr McFarlane had encouraged me to memorise the notes—and, whether or not it contributed much to my musicianship, the practice gave me great satisfaction.

When I returned to my seat after playing the Bach prelude, my father gave me a gentle dig with his elbow. 'You should have smiled,' he said, referring to the way I'd pursed my lips when I bowed at the audience. He was sweet, but he had no idea. Eisteddfods are the dog shows of amateur music: the judge evaluates each competitor for how well she conforms to the ideal standard of her breed, rewarding the winner for her proximity to an ideal that may well exist only in the judge's imagination. Rows of braces conformed to no adjudicator's ideal pianist.

The next competitor stood from her chair and walked to the stage, her long pale hair resting obediently behind her narrow shoulders. She wore a Laura Ashley paisley-print dress in swirling oceanic colours and a pair of knee-high brown boots that sported a one-inch heel. They may have been synthetic and rubber-soled, but those boots screamed sophistication to me, and they were the last thing my mother would think to buy. (Somehow I had become my toughest censor; I considered it out of the question to tell Mum what I really liked.) The girl's posture was so straight that it seemed as if she were not flesh and blood at all but carved from wood. She was as ideal an example of the young girl at the piano as if she had stepped out of Renoir's *Jeune filles au piano* series of the 1890s, porcelain skin and all. The image made flesh even had a French name: Jacqueline.

I looked down at my outfit of pants, short-sleeved cotton top and brown flats, embarrassed. As far as Mr McFarlane was concerned, my wardrobe was the major impediment to a career in music. A raised eyebrow greeted me one day when I showed up in a favourite pair of grey overalls; later I learned from another student of his that he had told her I'd turned up 'looking as if she'd just come in from the garden'. My piano lessons had been the last place I expected my sartorial decisions to be judged, especially by someone overly attached to polyester.

As Jacqueline walked slowly across the stage, I watched her every step, fascinated and envious. That kind of poise could not be taught. It could not be taught by Mr MacFarlane, at least. And certainly I had no poise of my own, with my utilitarian outfits, my braces, and eyebrows that threatened mutiny over the bridge of my nose—they looked like two unmown strips of lawn. I had yet to encounter Frida Kahlo's proud monobrow, but even if I had I'm pretty sure the discovery wouldn't have liberated me from my shame about my dark hair growing in places I didn't want it. Frida didn't have to turn up at school every day and face the blonde and hairless hordes: she and her massive eyebrow could just stay indoors and paint.

From the very first note Jacqueline played, she touched the keys with command and authority, and also with something that wasn't visible to the eye but more powerful for its intangibility. She played the same notes in the same order as I had, but the effect was transformed. There was an abiding sense of her deep connection to the work, as if she had seen through the signs and symbols printed on the page to the emotions roiling beneath the notation, and in her playing had conveyed her deep respect for the ocean as she sailed across the glittering water.

After the brief presto the prelude finishes with a six-bar coda that allows the pianist unusual freedom of expression and a variation of tempo between a slower adagio and returning to an allegro ending. Listening to the contrast between Jacqueline's presto and coda sections, I heard clearly the limitations of my own interpretation and wondered how it was that she and I could spend hours every week practising the piece, only for my performance to sound technically accurate but thin, as if I had only skimmed the surface.

The eisteddfod audience clapped politely as the last few competitors played through their Preludes and Fugues, but the result had already been decided. Jacqueline was so obviously Best in Show I couldn't figure out what was taking the adjudicator so long to announce the winner.

Finally the judge stood and cleared her throat. 'I'm going to award this one to Susan,' she declared to the hall of raised eyebrows, 'because she has played well all day.'

And what, I wondered, did that have to do with the price of fish? Woody Allen might be right that 80 per cent of success lies in simply showing up, but the remaining 20 per cent allows for a wide margin of error. Susan, a girl whose performance had been technically more competent than mine but equally bland, shook the judge's hand as my father rolled his eyes at me. He was already thinking of the long commute home from this parallel universe where alleged experts made us wait on uncomfortable seats for their irrational pronouncements. We were sitting inside a church, after all.

Susan held up her small trophy with an apologetic smile: everyone, including the winner, knew she didn't deserve it. Jacqueline had played all of us under our plastic chairs. I never saw her at another eisteddfod.

♫

Mr Jones strode into the assembly hall, his suit jacket billowing behind his long thin frame like the tail on a crotchet. He had been teaching music at Wenona for a long time, but no one knew how many years exactly; at our age time was as impossible to grasp as the twelve-tone scale.

I scuttled away from the grand piano, where I'd been playing 'Jessica's Theme' on request. Again.

But Mr Jones couldn't have cared less about my choice of material. He considered me neither talented nor exceptional, and endured my regular presence at the school's piano as any other condition of his ongoing employment.

'Apologies, girls. Forgot where we were meeting,' he muttered, dispensing each word as if it were coated in something sour. 'Come on, line up. We've wasted enough time already. If you don't have your music, stand next to someone who does. Virginia, go to the piano and play A, will you?'

A well-intentioned classmate piped up. 'She doesn't need the piano. She can just sing it like she does in madrigals.'

Anyone who has sung in a group knows that A is the note from which the singers work out the pitch of their respective first notes. Our weekly madrigals rehearsals, which were usually held in a basement room that had excellent acoustics but no piano, began with the choir mistress asking me to sound the starting note: my sense of pitch was so accurate that she didn't need a piano.

Mr Jones tilted his head slightly as he considered me, his black hawk eyes unblinking. After a pause, he said, 'You don't have perfect pitch.'

I shrugged, intuiting it was best to say nothing. Until Mrs Wilcox had suspected and tested my memory for pitch, I thought that everyone recognised notes by name as soon as they heard them. In the same way that most people can identify the colour of the sky or a fire engine, I can tell you what note almost any sound is, without reference to anything outside myself. I know, for example, that my printer spits out pages in a fuzzy C; the warning beep of the truck that reversed into a parking spot outside my window this morning is a B flat; and my doorbell's two-note chime is in the key of D major.

At school I considered this simply a freak of memory and took it for granted, not realising how unusual it was. My musicality seemed more like a curiosity than a practical asset—interesting, possibly, but useless. I didn't see how it might translate into something I could use in 'real life', which would begin promptly when I left this witches' cauldron and went to university.

'Go and stand over there, facing the wall,' said Mr Jones. 'Go on,' shooing me to the nearest side of the hall with one hand. At the cuffs of his shiny black suit was a permanent cloud formed by the stick of white chalk he gripped tightly and waved around like a poor man's baton during class.

He moved briskly to the piano. Moments before he'd been urging us to attention: now he had all the time in the world. My classmates, not knowing what was happening, sensed that it was nevertheless important and fell quiet. Even Joanna, whom I liked to think of as my best friend at school, began to pay attention.

Mr Jones played a note with one bony finger. It reverberated through the otherwise silent hall.

'B,' I said, straight away. My first mistake. Immediately I understood I should have waited a few seconds before responding. To at least pretend it took a conscious effort.

Mr Jones said nothing but pressed another note.

'E flat.' I couldn't help myself. The sound was as identifiable as my own face. I could no more pretend not to recognise each note than I could stop blinking. It wasn't my fault: absolute or perfect pitch is a genetic accident occurring in approximately one in ten thousand people.

Mr Jones increased the frequency of his note-playing and varied the register—playing some notes way up high on the keyboard and others low—but it made no difference to me.

'A, F sharp, B flat, D,' I shot back at him, emboldened. With every correct answer he stabbed the keys harder, as if the increasing violence of his dismay could change the pitch and catch me out. This was a game that would continue until Mr Jones decided it was over.

Without being able to see my classmates, I could only imagine their boredom. It was one thing for me to entertain them with show tunes and a medley of Top 40 songs; to be revealed to have a freak musical skill, beyond even the teacher's grasp, placed me in an entirely separate camp. Joanna wouldn't be pleased at my distinguishing myself in this way. My role as her friend was to remain on par with—or preferably slightly behind—her in intellectual and social achievement. She gave me my edge over her in Music as long as I didn't do better than her in Japanese, Economics and English. If recent history was a guide, she would ignore me for a few days until she decided I had been sufficiently punished for doing something she couldn't compete with.

Mr Jones shut the lid of the piano, and I returned to sit among my peers. But I had been cast out, and it was too late to return from wherever it was that I now found myself.

In 1839, in a letter to her aunt Elizabeth, the future novelist Mary Anne Evans (George Eliot) described a 'desire insatiable for the esteem of my fellow creatures' when playing the piano. She described this ambition punitively, as her 'besetting sin', fearing the power of her desire to perform for others. Her adolescence was characterised by an intense internal conflict: she sought praise but couldn't abide receiving it. Was it possible to be moral and to put oneself on public display? How does one reconcile the desire for admiration and the need to quench it? This is where shyness can become a tactic to disguise attention-seeking behaviour, a defence against being thought too aggressive and showy. To perform and then to agonise over it—especially if you're accomplished—is to remain suspended in a delicate balance between the poles of inner conflict. Rather an exhausting way of living, really.

I still wonder why Mr Jones wanted to disprove the fact that I had perfect pitch. Perhaps he felt outraged to learn that mere chance explained my consistently high marks in his classes, rather than his abilities as a teacher. Maybe he was furious that the unfairness of life was epitomised by an awkward fourteen-year-old girl who neither asked for nor appreciated her random gift. I wonder if Mr Jones somehow knew, his bitter gaze resting on the back of my white neck as I accurately named each note, that I would waste this ability; that I would abandon the piano and drift for years, casting about for an anchor as reliable and trustworthy as the starting note A.

10

This photograph of Alice May Morrison Taylor was taken in 1910 when it was well past September in Glasgow. Despite looking as if she's waiting for her children to come home from school, Alice has just turned fifteen.

While the bulky school uniform and cross-legged posture reveal little of her physically, I like to think this portrait tells us quite a lot about Alice as a teenager. She has taken great care with her appearance and her off-camera gaze, which calls attention to her creamy complexion and her partly open mouth. But is she expressing apology, surprise, boredom or impatience? Maybe it's just the awkwardness of not knowing how to relax in front of a camera, or how to be oneself in the careful quiet of the portrait photographer's studio. How staged and formal Alice's sombre comportment seems when you think of today's teenagers showing off their most flattering angles for ubiquitous cameras. The old convention of not smiling for a portrait photograph gives the impression that the subject led a life devoid of humour and colour—but that would be as false a conclusion as to interpret the beaming smiles of social media as literal 'happy' snaps.

Look at Alice's hair. That's a lot of hair for one head. Biologically speaking I didn't inherit mine from Alice so I can't blame her for it, but I wonder if she considered hers, as I came to view mine, equally blessing and curse. Her lustrous dark-brown tresses are arranged in some kind of complicated braiding, wound around her head with what looks like a network of pins. Did she construct that elegant bird's nest herself, or was it her mother's work? Of course I'm wondering if she had excess hair in places where she didn't want it, and whether she accepted it as God's will or devised home-made remedies to counteract a fuzzy upper lip.

When I turned fifteen I was yet to have a period, but seemingly overnight the Black Forest had marched all over my lily-white legs, making camp on the tops of my pale feet and even, the horror, my big toes. Coarse dark hair had crept along my upper thighs and over my abdomen, far north of where I'd always assumed the tree line would end. Long black strays had even appeared around my nipples like scouts from an advance party, which I yanked off with my hardworking tweezers. Monitoring the enemy was a covert operation requiring constant vigilance.

I was hirsute.

Hairy.

Hideous.

The models who reclined and cavorted in the glossy pages of *Dolly* magazine, which I consulted like a map of foreign territory, looked tanned and happy. Their teeth were straight. Their legs were smooth. There was no sign of hair around their bikini bottoms. Surreptitious surveillance of my classmates' limbs indicated that no one else had hair anywhere they didn't want it. In bed each night I prayed that if God would only turn back the advancing tide then I would definitely believe. In a recent class, Deborah Best had explained inflation, trade deficits and the Gross Domestic Product as easily as if she had already completed a four-year degree. My grasp of economics was less than solid, but a Gross Domestic Product was exactly how I thought of myself.

Aside from being a hairy horror, I had freckles on my face and arms, and braces on my teeth. I clearly grasped the meagre value of these assets in terms of how the law of supply and demand applied to a boy's interest in a girl.

The care Alice took to prepare for the portrait indicates a young woman very conscious of her body, even if she does not yet know what pleasures and betrayals it is capable of. The composition is so formal and contrived that it carries a slightly desperate whiff, as though the photographer, if not the subject herself, is determined to shape the future observer's impression of her. She is, if not a reader, then someone who wishes to be thought a reader. Or at least a reader of the King James Bible, the book she would have been most familiar with, seeing that there weren't many at home and Partick didn't get a public library until 1935.

It's an uncanny experience to gaze at Alice like this. In her unblemished face I recognise the old woman, though in photographs of an elderly Alice her teenage self is nowhere to be found. Perhaps a portrait will always be a kind of Rorschach test of the viewer's preconceptions, influenced by one's relationship to the subject. I wonder what Alice made of this portrait. Did it feel truthful to her, or a fiction composed for the eyes of others?

That Alice feels distant to me isn't so much a matter of time, though the photograph is now more than a century old. We've all had the experience of coming across photographs of strangers out of the past, thrust before your nose as you browse in the wooden boxes of a second-hand stall or antiques shop. In Alice's case I like to imagine she is holding herself back, pressing her real self like a cut flower behind the photographer's glass. By now she has been a soprano in the Dowanhill Church choir for three years. Once a week she takes a piano lesson with a Mrs Ramsay of 16 India Street, Partick. She would have paid for those lessons herself, most likely from her job in a haberdashery a few doors down Dumbarton Road, and perhaps she found the job in order to pay for the lessons.

I can only imagine how peaceful Mrs Ramsay's home must have been for Alice: an oasis compared to the formless symphony of knives and forks and cups and plates she practised in. That a woman could earn her living through the love of music would have been difficult for Alice to believe. Until she encountered Mrs Ramsay, Alice would have associated women's work with her mother's domestic rituals and with the mindless keeping of the haberdashery.

Did Alice consider herself lucky to have been born a woman? She never had to do the kind of physical labour that caused her father's bone-tiredness at the end of every day. Around the dinner table she must have noticed her brothers watching their father as they got older: seeing him, a mountain of a man, physically diminished by his job, recognising his lack of choice about how he earned the money that fed and housed them, and gradually understanding that their lives were likely to be variations on his theme.

The ambitious young woman in the portrait longs to be taken seriously. By now, though she is an increasingly visible figure in the musical life of her parish, I suspect that Alice nevertheless feels constrained by the yoke of her domestic responsibilities and a growing guilt. She must sense the gulf that is opening between what her parents expect of her and what she knows, with increasing certainty, that she wants. And what she wants is to live a life in which music plays a central rather than peripheral part. Though to all appearances Alice may strike the casual observer as a pious and reticent girl, she has a passionate intensity and capacity for playfulness that she has permitted only Nance, and occasionally her piano teacher, to see.

I like to think that when Alice first saw her photograph she was disappointed, because it captured her as the accommodating and secretive daughter she is at home. I look at

Alice as a young woman and think, *I would really like to understand you better.* And yet even as I recognise that desire, I suspect that whatever she felt most deeply either came out in her singing and playing, or remained silent.

II

I HAD A LOVE WHOSE NAME I dared not speak to my piano teacher: improvisation. The notes that weren't written down were the ones I loved best, the ones my fingers gravitated towards by default. But as Mr McFarlane's student, I diligently practised the works he'd chosen for that year's grade examination, in addition to the scales and arpeggios that were the foundation of any musician's study. As I was an advanced student heading towards the pointy end of eight examination grades, my daily practice comprised the constant repetition of the same notes in the same order.

My goal was a discernible improvement in accuracy and expression from one piano lesson to the next. Typically one section of each work needed special attention, whether it was clarifying the separate voices in a Bach fugue, perfecting a trill in a Beethoven sonata, or, in the case of Mozart—the composer who presented my greatest challenge—striking the balance between lightness of touch and emotional connection. Always with Mozart I felt defeated before I'd really begun to get the notes under my fingers; merely learning the right notes in the correct order was so far from what was necessary to fully convey the delicate beauty and formal perfection of a Mozart piano sonata, and I had neither the proper temperament nor sensibility to play it. I never felt that way with Beethoven, though his sonatas were no less of a technical challenge; nor with Bach, despite the demands of the fugues in particular. I felt a strange sense of kinship with Bach and Beethoven, which I never felt with Mozart. Kinship aside, the time I spent closely studying the works of those and other composers had made me realise how much I chafed on the limitations of faithfully respecting the fully notated score.

It was through my schedule as an accompanist that I became aware of my preference for improvising. Whenever I set a piece in front of me that wasn't for the purpose of examination, I regarded the accompaniment as a set of guidelines rather than a prescription. And even when the piece was a set work for study, I found myself straying from the music as notated, my fingers seeking out dissonance and delicious sounds made from notes that weren't written down. I spent hours by myself at the piano, tinkering with notes, playing with combinations of sounds that my ears heard as pretty, or ugly, or somewhere in between. Often an ugly sound made from a cluster of notes transformed into a gorgeous chord with the simplest of changes; one half-note's movement, a semitone up or down, was all it took. Perhaps ugly and beautiful were closer than I thought. Maybe any of us, whether we were beautiful or a nondescript and metal-mouthed maiden, were just a few notes away from thorough transformation.

Practising the second movement of a Mozart sonata, I would lose concentration and after ten minutes find my fingers tracing the patterns of my unconscious on the keyboard. Bored by repetition and rote learning, I thrilled to the variations I discovered by leaving everything to fingers and to chance—or probability, really, based on combinations made possible through the musician's working knowledge of harmony. Pianist Keith Jarrett, who built his reputation on solo performances of pure improvisation, said in a documentary that he learned he was an improviser by playing classical music. But I refused to embrace the same impulse. Each time I detoured from the notated music I felt guilty about it, as if I were a teenage boy who, having learned to play his own flute, can't help putting his hand down his pants.

On my way home from high school I often foraged at Allen's Music Store in Pitt Street, a vast emporium full of the nutrients essential to my piano diet. It was there that I had discovered the so-called Fake Books, a genre of cheap ring-bound editions that encourage the musician's departure from through-composed music. In fact, they assume the musician will use a Fake Book to learn a song's melody and harmonic structure, then depart from them to some degree in performance. Many of the titles in the Fake Books were drawn from the popular canon known as the American

Songbook. These songs—which originated on Broadway or in the dance-hall music of the early decades of the twentieth century—became what are known as jazz standards. These days the publications are known as Real Books, the difference being that the songs are now published with the copyright owners' permission.

When I brought home my first Fake Book, I was intimidated by the lack of visible notes, but soon realised how liberating it was to use a music chart instead of a notated score. The chord symbols were like a map that worked in reverse, wherever you found yourself: they revealed secrets of familiar territory hidden in plain sight, and made unfamiliar landscapes instantly recognisable. The freedom of finding my own notes to accompany a melody, to cast off from the notated shores, was exhilarating. By contrast with the fully notated music I'd studied so seriously for years, which made me feel like an automaton repeating an existing pattern of notes, these chord charts made me feel as though I was creating a new work from an existing shell—actively participating in a creative collaboration with the composer, rather than executing more or less accurately a replica of someone else's work. When performing classical music I was as necessarily disciplined and obedient to my soloist as a seeing-eye dog. But using the chord charts, I could vary the notes and as long as I stayed within the same key it made sense, musically speaking.

After three years of eisteddfod competition, I was yet to win. It hadn't occurred to me that I didn't excel because of my reservations about the rote learning of fully notated works. And yet everyone around me took my musicianship very seriously indeed. Mr McFarlane spoke to me as if I were a real musician who had a professional future. At school my teachers and classmates applauded my solo performances. My proud parents sang my praises to anyone who would listen. I wasn't complaining, but for some reason I couldn't trust their judgement. A born sceptic, I assumed my piano teacher was paid to take me seriously, that my school lacked other precocious pianists to compare me to, and that my parents neither wanted nor sought third-party validation for their loving compliments. I felt like a toddler praised for sliding down a slippery dip when all I believed I'd done was obey the laws of gravity. Playing the piano came easily to me, I reasoned, in the same way that other girls swam fast or attracted boys. It felt like a natural affinity that had emerged with the good fortune of domestic encouragement and expert teaching, more than something I was actively pursuing on my own behalf. My career in classical piano music had come to feel, in short, like a performance in and of itself. In getting close to but never reaching the pinnacle of eisteddfod success, I confirmed my suspicion that while I might be highly competent, I was far from exceptional.

Having grown tired of my Highly Commended certificates and runner-up trophies, I decided it was time to come out about my preference for syncopation and flattened seventh notes. I asked Mr McFarlane if I could enter the Jazz Instrumental section of this year's competition. Wanting to win, I hoped I would fare better in this section because there were fewer competitors. And if I had been honest with myself, with my teacher, with my parents, or anyone else for that matter, I would have admitted that I cared more for Brubeck, Ellington, Gershwin and the Australian jazz singer-songwriter Vince Jones than I did for the Mozart sonata I was also performing in competition.

There was a long pause while Mr McFarlane digested my question. I was usually as inscrutable as the Sphinx, and had never asked him for anything before. 'What piece would you like to play?' he said, eventually.

I didn't hesitate. '"Blue Rondo à la Turk" by Dave Brubeck.'

'From *Time Out*?'

Now it was my turn to be surprised. Released in 1959, *Time Out* was an album of original compositions in unconventional time signatures. The critics disliked it immediately, and it became the first jazz album to sell one million copies. It reached number two on the Billboard 1961 pop album chart, and the album's famous track 'Take Five' made it to twenty-five on the Billboard Top 100 in October that year. Perhaps my teacher did not, as I had assumed, listen only to Brahms and Beethoven.

I had bought a book of Brubeck compositions from Allen's Music Store, whose jazz section was like my social life at the time: small and frequently empty. The broader reaches of

Allen's printed music aisles were only slightly more populated, dotted with young men whose faces were in turn dotted with pimples. If only I'd been able to join the dots and smile in their general direction, I'd have had something to do on a Saturday night. But just as the solitary giant panda subsists strictly on the soft shoots of the bamboo tree, I grazed in the piano section, sniffing out musical morsels. With my pocket money I bought the two-volume Edition Peters set of Beethoven piano sonatas, feeling triumphant at finally being able to return my teacher's copy. But it was acquiring a prized example of the late twentieth-century piano repertoire—the collected works of Billy Joel, in three tasty volumes—that really made my mouth water. And like the pandas, I wasn't interested in mating: my promiscuity manifested only in an insatiable appetite for new music to sight-read.

The glossy cover of *Jazz Masters: Dave Brubeck* featured an extreme close-up of his face washed in a deathly blue that did nothing to make the grey-haired fifty-something pianist seem any younger. Were it not for the fact that the book contained my only access to a notated version of 'Blue

Rondo', the composer's looming countenance would have been sufficient reason to avoid going anywhere near it. Instead I took it home, where I was forced to look at him several times daily whenever I opened or shut the book during practice.

In Mr McFarlane's studio we listened to 'Blue Rondo' on a cassette player to ensure consistency between the music on the page and the recorded version. As an approach to playing jazz music, imitating a great player is the stuff of training wheels, but I had to start somewhere. While I sat beside my teacher, I wanted to nod my head, move my shoulders and bounce my knees, but my instinct—however mistaken—told me to remain perfectly still. It was excruciating, and not just because of Mr McFarlane's body odour.

The piece is composed primarily in 9|8 time, a rhythmic meter I hadn't encountered in any classical repertoire. Nine fast beats per bar are divided into a rapid-fire *one-two one-two one-two one-two-three.* Then every fourth bar the feeling changes to a more waltz-like *three plus three plus three* in 3|4 time. Brubeck had based the piece on a traditional rhythm he'd heard street musicians play when he was touring in Turkey. 'It's like the blues to you, 9|8 is to us,' Turkish musicians in Istanbul told him.[39] Like any jazz composition, it's a structure made for improvising, its purpose to drive variation and playfulness in performance.

There was one fundamental flaw in the very idea of the Jazz Instrumental competition at the eisteddfod: it depended on the competitors performing notated music. The event involved no improvisation whatsoever.

♫

'There's never been a time when improvisation has been given the respect it deserves,' said jazz pianist Keith Jarrett in 2005. A jazz musician best known for his completely improvised solo concerts could be expected to be a little irritated with a recent lack of respect in the music world, but Jarrett's view was short-sighted. Improvisation is still ubiquitous throughout the world, just not in most types of music given serious critical attention in the West. Jazz was shunned by the academy until graduate programs were established in the latter decades of the twentieth century;

freestyle rap is perhaps musical improvisation's most popular current form.

We celebrate musicians of mythology, forgetting they were all improvisers. Name the tune Orpheus performed to rescue Eurydice from the dead. Or the music Pan played to enchant his followers. And which composer helped the Pied Piper lure the children of Hamelin over the nearest cliff? Their music wasn't notated or available for purchase or download. Their life-changing acts of music-making didn't differentiate performance from composition. The stories of Orpheus, Pan and the Pied Piper reflect the world of music as it was for most of its history—musicians invented it as they played their instruments, or they experimented with variations of melodies they had picked up along their travels, without regard to precise notation or copyright. Musicians composed while they performed: in other words, they improvised.

In 1829, a decade prior to his *Letters to a Young Lady*, Czerny wrote a book entitled *The Art of Improvisation.* Fifty years after Nannerl Mozart dazzled her father with her spontaneous creativity, it was now expected that virtuosi improvise preludes to the works on their recital programs, to extemporise (an interchangeable term) on given themes or familiar tunes, and to invent cadenzas (codas) to works during performance.

One early student of *The Art of Improvisation* was ten-year-old Clara Wieck, whose piano performances during the 1830s regularly featured her improvisations. Touring with his adolescent prodigy, Frederick Wieck wrote to his wife that 'No one could believe that she could compose, since that has never been true of girls of her age, and when she improvised on a given theme, all were beside themselves.' On another occasion he boasted: 'Clara, as a girl, already has an advantage over all the female pianists in the world, in that she can improvise.'[40] By the time she became her century's greatest woman pianist, improvisation had been part of public performance for two centuries, and Clara was considered one of the greatest exponents.[41]

Czerny believed that any amateur pianist could learn how to improvise, as long as she had attained a 'more than moderate skill in playing'. It wasn't a specialised skill set of the elite virtuoso musician and the concert hall, but rather an approach to music, a way of playing almost any instrument, that many amateurs could share. In *Letters to a Young Lady*, Czerny described extemporising as playing that 'which has neither been written down before, nor previously prepared or studied, but which is merely the fruit of a momentary and accidental inspiration'.[42] He encouraged his ideal student Cecilia to attempt to 'connect together easy chords, short melodies, passages, scales, arpeggioed chords, or which is much better, leave it to your fingers to effect this connection, according to their will and pleasure'.

But, typically of a creative act that gave women a channel for self-expression, the practice of improvisation triggered ambivalent responses. Not even Clara Schumann could count on the support of her husband in the practice. 'One word of advice,' he wrote her, 'don't improvise too much; too much gets away that could be put to better use. Resolve always to get everything down on paper right away.'[43] Thus does the document trump the improvisation, the composer the improviser.

As a teenager, Clara did compose. 'Composing gives me great pleasure,' she declared in 1853. 'There is nothing that surpasses the joy of creation, if only because through it one wins hours of self-forgetfulness, when one lives in a world of sound.'[44] But she didn't perform her own compositions during concerts as her contemporary Liszt did, or as Bach, Beethoven and Mozart had done before her. She suffered from too much self-doubt. At the ripe old age of twenty, when we are nowhere near wise beyond our years, she decided to abandon it. 'I once believed that I possessed creative talent, but I have given up this idea,' she wrote. 'A woman must not desire to compose—there has never yet been one able to do it. Should I expect to be the one?'

Instead, Clara introduced into concert programming the idea of performing other composers' works. In her Vienna debut in 1837, for example, the nineteen-year-old presented Beethoven's piano sonatas to a concert audience in their entirety for the first time—ten years after the composer's death.[45] Clara made this practice her own as she performed all over Europe for decades to come; it was her choice, but her promotion of the works of older male composers exerted enormous influence over the format of concerts that persists today. By the mid-nineteenth century, works by dead composers dominated the concert halls of Europe. The acrobatic hijinks of virtuoso pianists such as Franz Liszt (who studied as a child prodigy with Czerny) presenting their own compositions gave way to the model of performers who focused on interpreting the works of others.[46] In this genre of music, the separation of creator and performer was all but complete.

By century's end, improvisation had gone out of fashion. This attitude is reflected in Kate Chopin's 1899 novel *The Awakening*. Chopin takes a dim view of the elderly Mademoiselle Reisz improvising, describing how she 'sat low at the instrument, and the lines of her body settled into ungraceful curves and angles that gave it an appearance of deformity'.

The development of the classical repertoire, and the music publishing industry that burgeoned and profited from it, depended on notation. Improvisation disappeared from performance, replaced by literal adherence to the music as written. My piano transcription of Brubeck's *Time Out* recording exemplified the attempt to commodify a type of performance—specifically designed for spontaneous creativity—that was anathema to full notation. The twentieth-century amateur could be forgiven for considering the written music as Scripture, as if from the beginning there had been the Notes.

♫

Judging the Jazz Instrumental competition was a conductor best known for leading the TV studio orchestra in a daytime variety show. The Maestro was a short man with a bowl-cut carpet of black hair and an impassive expression.

Having grown out of the habit of wearing pants, I performed 'Blue Rondo à la Turk' in a flared forest-green skirt with a wide self-belt, paired with an apricot-coloured short-sleeved fitted cotton top. What can I say? It was the 1980s.

'Her performance . . . was a startling one; the forte pedal was held down throughout; the big chords were crashed and banged with all the strength a pair of twelve-year-old arms could put into them; and wrong notes were freely scattered. Still, rhythm and melody were well marked, and there was no mistaking the agility of the small fingers.'

This vivid description is not of me but of Laura Rambotham, Henry Handel Richardson's schoolgirl heroine from her 1910 novel, *The Getting of Wisdom*. Laura is giving a spirited rendition of a difficult work by Thalberg, Mozart's contemporary, for her humourless headmistress—a fictional equivalent of my equally humourless Maestro. But the physical effort Laura puts into the Thalberg reminds me of the energy it took me to perform the Brubeck, with its chord clusters and its rapid switches between time signatures.

With my bare arms flailing and my heels tapping, I gradually formed the impression, however, that my enjoyment at playing 'Blue Rondo' was a lot greater than my audience's pleasure in listening to it. I'm not sure what specifically gave me that idea; such thoughts run on the intangible currents between performer and audience. And it was difficult to know what precisely the problem could be, let alone how I could do anything to fix it. Was it that the piece was unknown to the audience and therefore faced invisible resistance? Was the composition too strange with its abrupt rhythmic changes? Too Turkish-sounding—whatever that meant? Or was it simply too contemporary by eisteddfod standards, at only twenty-five or so years old at the time?

Perhaps I should have selected a Gershwin or Duke Ellington number with more whiskers on it, as several other competitors had. After I finished, as I smiled and bowed and left the stage, I wondered why it never occurred to me to do something straightforward.

Returning to my seat, I noticed the Maestro staring at me with a puzzled look. I hoped he was impressed with my choice of material. No other competitor had selected such a rhythmically complicated work.

So as the Maestro handed out the awards and I remained empty-handed, I was more than a little disappointed. In fact I was dumbfounded: I may not have been the people's choice, but I couldn't imagine how I had failed to persuade him. Laura Rambotham had felt proud of how she'd played the Thalberg, but later found herself accused of a 'gross impertinence, in profaning the ears' of the other guests, and learned that she should have played Mozart instead.

As I stood to collect my things, the Maestro appeared beside me with my *Jazz Masters: Dave Brubeck* book. At the sight of Brubeck beaming from the cover, my hopes lifted. In my defeat I had forgotten to retrieve it. Perhaps the judge would utter some terse words of encouragement.

'I must tell you that you had the rhythm of that piece all wrong,' he said, lips pursed, as he handed me the book. 'I just thought I should let you know.'

Laura Rambotham herself could not have been more surprised. Had the Maestro not once heard *Time Out*? It was quite possible I hadn't played 'Blue Rondo' as well as I thought I had, but rhythmically I had played it like Brubeck does on his own recording. I could accept an adjudicator not caring for my playing—that had largely been the story of my eisteddfod career. But it was on Brubeck's behalf that I was outraged. For once I didn't blame myself for my failure: I diagnosed the Maestro with a severe case of arrhythmia.

12

Alice played one note at a time on the church piano, the first of each broken chord the choir sang arpeggio. Their voices, ascending in unison then falling as they returned to the home note, had the comforting roll of water lapping the shore. For three years now she had led the choir's midweek rehearsals and warm-ups on Sundays before the service.

From her first solo soprano part at a Sunday service, Alice's clear articulation and honeyed tone had lifted the whole choir out of what a few newer members might have characterised as complacency. Despite his frail appearance, old Mr Somerville's ears were still as sharp as those of the youngest tenor in his charge. He made a point of complimenting Alice in front of the choir after that service, and his brief encouragement lit a fire beneath her vocal ambitions. She had been surprised by her confidence in singing in front of an audience, the way that she felt uninhibited and utterly herself. More so than she did almost anywhere except whispering with Nance in their room before they fell asleep each night. On a stage she was Alice May Morrison Taylor, the pious young woman with the bell-like soprano voice, who loved her family and God and the music of worship, though not necessarily in that order.

Like the rest of the congregation at Dowanhill United Free Church, Alice had been nervous at the news of Frederick Hervey's taking up the position of choirmaster on Mr Somerville's retirement. Hervey's reputation as a severe taskmaster preceded him. According to an article about him in the Musical Herald, *Mr Hervey was a teaching member of the Tonic Sol-fa College, Singing Master of Renfrew School Board, a lecturer and music master at the Bible Training Institute of Glasgow, Music Master of Girls' Orphan Homes at Whiteinch, Conductor of the Scotstoun Male Voice Choir, and Musical Director of Windsor Halls Church in Glasgow. Alice marvelled at how one man could hold down so many jobs, but her mother was dismissive. 'He's in everything but a bath,' she said.*

Now that Alice had left school and was working full-time in Mrs Rankin's haberdashery, she could afford both piano and voice lessons. Under Mr Somerville's choir leadership, she had flourished into a key member of the soprano section and an occasional soloist. Mr Hervey offered her a discounted rate for private singing lessons with him in return for her help in leading the rehearsals. It became her responsibility to plan them, to ensure the choristers had the music they needed when they needed it, and to liaise with Gardner Street and Windsor Halls, the other major Glaswegian churches at which the Dowanhill choir performed in the major concerts of each year. Alice considered the responsibility a pleasure, reflecting the esteem in which she hoped she was held.

Even so, she chafed at the constraints her teacher placed on her vocal technique. During her first lesson, Alice—quietly proud of her God-given tone and her lung capacity—sang her warm-up arpeggios as if she were performing them. After she finished, Mr Hervey looked at her for a long moment. In the silence Alice heard her hubris. 'You have great natural talent,' he said, finally. 'A good ear, a good range, and a lovely rich tone,' he added. 'But you're in a hurry, and musicianship is not a race.'

While she enjoyed playing the piano at church, Alice had come to find practising the instrument repetitive and, though she would never have admitted it to dear old Mrs Ramsay, horribly dull. Alice wondered now whether her feelings for the piano were like the love a mother might have for a child who was adopted rather than born of her own flesh, which is how she now thought of her voice. And yet here was Mr Hervey, taking her back to the beginning, to the most rudimentary aspects of singing. He drilled her with exercises in basic voice production and building lung capacity. He paid inordinate attention to her posture, and his approach to phrasing was nothing short of painstaking.

'A singer is in the unique position of being both the instrument and the performer,' he would say. 'We need to get you singing from the inside out, singing with your whole body.' Alice, intimidated at the very idea of her body's involvement in the sounds she sang, did not understand what he meant but trusted that in time she would. Despite her impatience, the brief hour that she spent each week with Mr Hervey studying melody and harmony, phrasing and pitch, was what she looked forward to most.

Mr Hervey's working life, immersed in music, seemed a magical existence to Alice when contrasted with the oil and grime of her father's lot, and her grim tenement home where there was love but little music. She drank in her teacher's stories of his time as a student at the Royal Academy in London, of attending several concerts each week, and of the talented women who were now training at the Guildhall School to conduct small choirs.

Sometimes, in her more extravagant daydreams, Alice pictured herself walking the streets of London and attending the Guildhall, but the idea was as far-fetched as some of the novels she had read. Fictional young ladies travelled to Europe to study music as if it were the most normal thing for a girl to do. Having never heard of such impossible extravagance outside the pages of these novels, Alice quickly tired of them. Just once she wanted to read the story of a plain girl from a working-class family who made a life for herself using her musical talent that didn't involve marrying or being born into the right family. In too many books all roads led to weddings—unions that produced babies and turned the mother from her piano (it was always a piano) into an exhausted slave.

Nance couldn't understand Alice's heretical views, but then Alice always had been the practical sister. Just as she could read instantly the shape of the songs she sang, Alice could see the landscape of relationships between men and women, even if her only experience of such relationships was that of the observer. She preferred the routines of piano practice and choir rehearsal to her mundane domestic duties. How she and Nance could have been raised in the same household and drawn such different conclusions about the realities of married life, Alice did not know.

'You just wait. You'll feel differently when you meet the right one,' her sister would say.

Everyone was always telling her to wait. It was too easy to remind Nance that as a pretty girl she could pick and choose among her admirers, and had been doing just that for several years before Richard turned up at church one day like the answer to a redundant prayer. Other girls thought about putting things into a glory box, but Alice couldn't see the point if she was to dedicate herself to music: glory boxes were for the girls to whom young men paid attention and who looked forward to marriage.

Nance and Richard's decision to emigrate to Australia came as a disappointing surprise to their parents, who had been looking forward to tripping over a brood of grandchildren. 'I wish you'd be happy for me,' Nance sobbed as they farewelled each other at Partick Station.

Alice, despite having been privy to the newlyweds' decision, failed to muster any joy for her sister's good fortune. Instead she chided herself for her feelings of loss and worried that she would never replace her only confidante. With Nance embarking on a new life, Alice could not help but wonder whether there would ever be someone special she might sing for in her own future.

13

It was always a relief to play the school Steinway, to feel the smooth keys beneath my fingertips and the sustain pedal beneath my right foot, and to hear the notes as they sound and know I produced them. Away from the piano, my flat chest and pale freckled skin made me feel invisible, but when I sat down at the instrument I somehow grew taller and more powerful in my seat, as if I were riding a horse sixteen hands high and could see and hear everything.

And did those feet in ancient times . . .

I didn't mind playing 'Jerusalem' yet again. My job was straightforward: read the music, translate that through my fingertips into black and white keys as it was written, and play at a consistent speed so the whole school could sing along, and at a volume where everyone felt confident about raising their voices and keeping them aloft. I understood the piano—its vocabulary, its technical capabilities and its emotional range—and enjoyed the power at my fingertips. How easy it was to help the singers find the note they needed, so subtly they didn't even know I was helping them, or to confuse them in an instant if I chose. If I were to stop suddenly, so would everybody else. Even Miss Jackson. I could induce an instant silence in hundreds of girls, though silence was always the last thing I wanted to hear. It was comforting to feel I could control one thing in my life, when so much of the rest of it was out of my hands. I was the captain of this ship, if only for a few precious minutes.

In 1832, when George Eliot was a thirteen-year-old student at Miss Franklin's school at Coventry, she was considered 'the best performer in the school'. But the teenaged Mary Anne Evans felt highly ambivalent about her skills at the piano. A recollection of her as a highly musical thirteen-year-old student describes her sensitivity as 'painfully extreme'. She would dutifully perform for visitors 'though suffering agonies from shyness and reluctance', then 'rush to her room and throw herself on the floor in an agony of tears'.[47]

My own extreme sensitivity was the opposite of Eliot's, occurring away from the piano rather than at it. I might worry about making a mistake, but it was one I could cover, and later I would practise to ensure I'd never make it again. But away from the piano, one error could result in death of the irrevocable, social kind.

At the piano I glanced up at the most senior students, warbling from the upper storey of the assembly hall. I hoped that in a year or so, when I reached their age, I would have their curves as well as their confidence. It was all very well being able to perform a Mozart sonata from memory or play a new piece at first sight, but what did it matter if you weren't invited to parties and didn't know any boys? Earlier that year my friend Joanna had shunted me out of the way as soon as she met Matthew at one of those parties. With her boyfriend, her shoulder-length blonde hair and her eye-popping breasts, Joanna had entered a social orbit in which mysterious friends outside our school, who knew boys of similar ages to us, hosted parties that those boys attended. An orbit to which I, with my braces, monobrow and inconvenient location, was denied access.

Playing through 'Jerusalem' by rote, I thought about how pathetic and ugly I was. I couldn't blame Joanna for tiring of me. While she had become a woman, I had remained stuck in girlhood, practising my piano. Joanna's cheeks teemed with huge white-headed pimples, but Matthew still wanted to kiss her. There must be more to the business of being a woman than I knew. It couldn't have been just my braces or hairy legs—something else must be wrong with me. Maybe it was because I had perfect pitch.

I will not cease from Mental Fight,
Nor shall my sword sleep in my hand:
Till we have built Jerusalem,
In Englands green & pleasant Land.

As Joanna never invited me over to her house anymore, and told me nothing about what she and Matthew did at weekends, I concluded that beside attending the occasional party they did nothing but have sex. In the words of 'Jerusalem', they had built their own green and pleasant land, in which his sword did everything in her hand but sleep. Leaving me with the ceaseless mental fight, a struggle that was both endless and already lost.

It wasn't so long ago that Joanna and I had made each other laugh so hard that tears ran down our cheeks and we gasped for breath. When we swooned over Paul Weller and spent weekend afternoons repetitively playing his Style Council albums. When we watched crude Mel Brooks movies and invented sexual fantasies for our prim grey-haired English teacher Miss Anderson, whom we were convinced was still a virgin like we were.

Like I was.

Marianne Dashwood in Jane Austen's *Sense and Sensibility* was the girl after my own broken heart: 'She spent whole hours at the pianoforte alternately singing and crying; her voice often totally suspended by her tears.' When she wasn't miserable at the piano, Marianne was miserable with a book in her hand: 'In books too, as well as in music, she courted the misery which a contrast between the past and present was certain of giving.' At home the piano was the perfect location for me to wallow in self-pity. I could have a good cry about how unhappy I was at school, keeping my back to the rest of the house. I took comfort from the pent-up tears inching down my cheeks, knowing that the only other place I could do this safely was the shower. Despite the noise-absorbent shag pile under my feet, I was attuned to the warning sounds of an approaching parent, which gave me time to drag the back of my hand across my eyes and apply my happy face.

Marianne Dashwood's thoughts as she cried, played and read were purer than mine. The idea of sex fascinated and revolted me, and I couldn't stop thinking about it. The third verse of 'Jerusalem' was teeming with phallic references: a bow of burning gold, arrows of desire—even a spear, for goodness' sake. It was amazing that Miss Jackson allowed us to sing the hymn at all. Did Joanna and Matthew do it in bed? Did they lie under the sheet or on top of the duvet? On a couch with an old towel laid down first, or in a secluded park under a blanket and a hollowed-out tree?

When they kissed, how did they breathe? Wasn't she afraid of becoming pregnant? How would you even put on a condom? Maybe she was on the pill. But how did she get to the doctor without her mother knowing? Did Matthew's thingy stand up straight or stick out? Did she kiss it? If she did, didn't it smell? How did they clean up all the goo that must go everywhere? In *Dolly* magazine I'd read references to a mysterious 'wet patch'. It sounded disgusting.

After four verses, 'Jerusalem' finally came to an end. 'Thank you, Victoria,' Miss Jackson said. I should have been pleased at her mistaking me for someone else, yet again, but as much as I longed to disappear at the piano, I depended on it as the one thing that helped me to stand out. Our principal's misattributed gratitude was as reliable as her admonitions against eating in public and applauding in church, activities that she considered equally *vulgar.* Just as well she wasn't a mind-reader—she'd have had a conniption at my filthy imaginings.

In November 1838, after hearing an oratorio performed by the Choral Union in Coventry, George Eliot described her complicated feelings about being an accomplished musician in a letter to her dear friend and former teacher, the evangelical Miss Lewis. 'It would not cost me any regrets if the only music heard in our land were that of strict worship,' she began piously, though she immediately qualified her enjoyment: 'nor can I think a pleasure that involves the devotion of all the time and powers of an immortal being to the acquirement of an expertness in so useless (at least in ninety-nine cases out of a hundred) an accomplishment, can be quite pure or elevating in its tendency'. A very wordy way of saying that to give pleasure by performing music is an accomplishment that takes god-like dedication and skill, but is pointless. That's nothing if not ambivalent.

In Jane Austen's *Persuasion*, Anne Elliot finds solitude and privacy at the piano while she accompanies others dancing (including Captain Wentworth, whose engagement she had broken off eight years earlier), 'and though her eyes would sometimes fill with tears as she sat at the instrument, she was extremely glad to be employed, and desired nothing in return but to be unobserved'. To be useful, and to be left alone: I suspect that was the true goal of my high school music career. This is where George Eliot got the wrong end of the stick about performing for an audience: it isn't an appeal for attention, but rather a defensive strategy in which your instrument functions as an effective tool of border protection. The piano in fact affords you great privacy. At the piano you do not have to engage in conversation. You do not have to risk saying the wrong thing. You sit at your instrument for a reason; you are there for active purpose. Not to be looked at per se, as if you were posing awkwardly for your portrait.

Despite her rejection of me, I still believed reviving Joanna's friendship to be a worthy goal. In his *Letters to a Young Lady*, Czerny wrote: 'There is no higher satisfaction than in being able to distinguish one's self before a large company, and in receiving an honourable acknowledgement of one's diligence and talent.' But Czerny was wrong. I had received a bucketload of honourable acknowledgement, but as far as I was concerned the higher satisfaction would be to have Joanna's friendship again. And maybe a boyfriend.

14

In March 1914, Alice May Morrison Taylor won a First Class Certificate of Merit at the annual competition of the Scottish National Song Society, held in Glasgow. According to her certificate, she scored 90 out of a possible 100 for 'quality, expression, time and tune, general affect, voice, expression, and general conception'. In her first outing at the competition the previous year, she had scored a mere 85. The quality of her singing made her eligible for the National Sangschaw, the competitive pinnacle of Scottish music, poetry and song; she came home with one gold and one silver medal.

Who can say what Alice's parents made of her exemplary musicianship. But after repeated success in competition, and regular performances around Glasgow, she must have allowed herself to dare hope for something more than a job in Mrs Rankin's haberdashery. She must by then have come to think of herself as a musician, feeling confident in her skills and expertise, and their usefulness to church choirs in her home town. Surely she would have aspired to a professional life in music. How else to explain the existence of this letter, written by her teacher, Frederick Hervey, dated 19 May 1914:

> *This letter certifies that Alice May Morrison Taylor has studied singing with me for the past two years, gaining first class certificates of merit at the 1913 and 1914 Scottish Song Society (with marks of 85 and 90 out of a possible 100, respectively). She has a soprano voice of good quality and range: reaching to A above the score and G below. She sings with good taste and perception and her frequent public appearances have been well spoken of by the press. Her extensive repertoire includes Handel's* Messiah *and* Theodora. *She is*

a very painstaking and enthusiastic musician and I have great pleasure in recommending her for any important appointment she may seek.

Not long after, Alice accepted the position of choirmistress at the larger and more prestigious Gardner Street Church, an appointment that reflects her rising stature in the musical life of Glasgow even more than the influence of her respected teacher.

15

Five hundred people settled into their seats inside the Hunters Hill Town Hall and waited for the lights to dim. The philanthropically minded folk of the neighbourhood had gathered for a concert to celebrate the opening night of the Rotary Club charity art show, which my father had been coordinating, in addition to the charity golf day, for ten years. He specialised in thankless annual events. My participation as a featured soloist tonight was voluntary too. My specialty was playing the piano in public, an activity I was no longer sure I enjoyed.

While I sat at one side of the front row waiting to walk on stage, my clammy palms felt as porous as the honey-coloured sandstone from which the hall had been built in 1866. With several minutes still to go before I was due to perform, I was trying to visualise the opening bars of the piece I was about to play from memory: it was in Book Four of the *Mikrokosmos*, a work that Béla Bartók composed from 1926 to 1939. Recalling pieces note for note had always been a point of pride for me. I could play a Mozart or Beethoven sonata of ten minutes' duration without forgetting a thing. Usually I summoned the score instantly in my mind's eye, but tonight, for the first time in my junior performance career, I couldn't remember how the piece began. Which was ironic given that Bartók felt no shame about performing his own music in public with the score.[48]

You'll be fine, you'll remember how it begins when you get up there, I told myself, calling my own bluff as I walked on stage to generous applause. Many of those clapping enthusiastically had watched me grow up at the piano. Just beyond the stage lights I could make out Mr and Mrs Kovacek, whose son went to school with my brother; they had announced their separation years earlier but never went through with it due to the expense of divorce. In front of them sat the Bickersons, a codename my brother and I used for a Rotarian and his wife who argued constantly in front of others. Closer to the front the mayor's glamorous wife sat beside her husband wearing makeup applied like a coat of armour. Her look was all blonde streaks and sequins, an Australian translation of the hit television series *Dynasty*. Her razor-sharp shoulderblades threatened the spaghetti straps of her sleeveless shift.

I nodded and smiled into the constellation of faces, then sat in front of the huge Kawai grand piano I had rehearsed on earlier that afternoon. My hair, cut in a long bob that fell over half my face, hid the evidence plainly written on it. For once I had defied my mother, who still insisted I pull it back into a ponytail. 'So everyone can see your face,' she'd said. Again.

Through the unconscious knowledge of trained muscles, the opening of the Bartók miraculously came to me. On stage I exhaled slowly, recognising that this was yet another occasion when there had been no need for me to fret as much as I had. I'd been foolish to let my imagination run away with catastrophic scenarios.

I was about two-thirds of the way through when I became aware of my hands hovering over the keys. It took me less than half a second to realise that I didn't know what came next. My mind's eye, which had always automatically scrolled through the printed music, had failed to turn the page.

I shook my wrists slightly as if this would jump-start my memory, but nothing changed. I couldn't recall what followed all the notes I had just played, nor could I experiment while hundreds of ears were tuned in my direction. In life I was often at a loss for words, but at the piano I had never lost the next note. My hands paused in midair, I heard the silence emanating from the hundreds of people watching me.

As there was no apparent way forward, the only thing I could do was to go back. To the beginning. I started all over again, part of me wondering how many in the audience even noticed I had done so in their relief that I had broken the spell of my silence.

I was grateful for the curtain of hair that fell across my face. I couldn't see anyone, not least my mother. She might not have picked up on what was happening musically but would still be wishing I'd at least worn a barrette.

Working my way towards the part where I had lost all sense of direction minutes earlier, I felt an unexpected rush at having given over to my fingers the responsibility of getting me home—as if, after being paralysed in combat, the only available course of action was to trust my comrades to carry me to safety. Whether muscle memory would kick in this time, I would simply have to wait and see.

Before I knew it I was playing the last third, flying toward the final bars knowing freedom lay immediately beyond them. For long seconds, my heart in my mouth, I'd considered my options if memory had failed me again. There were none. Like Houdini I had survived a situation in which I'd had no option other than to escape, or to die on stage.

When my hands finally came to a stop I paused over the keys to emphasise that both performer and audience had reached the end of the sorry saga. I stood up to rapturous applause in which I heard the vibrato of relief.

After the concert, by the trestle tables laden with self-serve tea and coffee and Arnott's Assorted biscuits, I smiled and shrugged at a succession of well-meaning people as they congratulated me on my death-defying performance. I responded on autopilot to the whos, hows, whys and whats from old women and older men. Why was Rotarianese so easy for me to speak, I wondered, when I struggled to talk about anything interesting with most girls my age? Because of my intensive piano study and furtive improvisations I often felt older than my peers, but I was too young to be so comfortable with the people who surrounded me now, who really were old. At fifteen I still hadn't had a period or a boyfriend. Old could wait.

16

In the summer of 1917, the light of Glasgow blinked weakly through the long days, as if even the sun were drained from the years of war. People ground down by fear and loss hungered for beauty, for a reminder that it was sometimes possible still to enjoy life. And so they turned out in their hundreds to hear again the familiar soprano voice that belonged to one of their own.

The audience at Windsor Halls Church was three times the size of that at any of Alice May Morrison Taylor's recent concerts. Tonight the crowd included the soloist's parents, whose enthusiasm for their daughter's musicianship had dimmed in proportion to her growing public profile and critical regard. Nevertheless Mr and

Mrs Taylor were proud to attend Alice's recital this evening in the company of their son Vincent, home for a few weeks while HMS Mameluke *underwent repairs in the nearby docks.*

Singing in public, Alice still felt alive in a way that she did nowhere else. On stage she was in control of her voice, she knew her repertoire, and she felt prepared. She welcomed the jolts of anxiety that arrived before each performance as a reminder that singing for others was what she loved best. It was the one time in her life when she was the centre of attention. And while she avoided standing out from the crowd when she was among them, Alice felt completely at home on stage with all eyes trained upon her. There really was nothing like the presence of an audience.

Every time she walked onto a stage and stood silently while the polite welcome applause faded, Alice felt an almost erotic charge. The warm embrace of the spotlight. The undivided attention of strangers. The exquisite quiet just before the conductor lifted his baton, or her accompanist's fingers touched the keyboard. Alice had grown up in an endless river of noise: her brothers' scrabbling play inside the house, the clatter of cutlery and the percussion of pots and pans, and her father's voice booming like a tuba from one end of the narrow tenement to the other. The 502 tram and horse-drawn carts rattling along Dumbarton Road, the distant toll of church bells, the piercing shrieks of trains. And the occasional bellowing of new ships from the Clyde as they departed for the shores of a war that seemed it would never end.

Some members of the audience, surveying the soprano's modest home-made silk gown of pale grey—and not for the first time—might have wished she had found for herself a nice young man by now. But even had she been able to show off a waist and a charming smile, luck would still have been against her. Outside the measures of a music score, Alice's timing was poor. So many of those eligible for the role of husband were either playing their part in the North Sea or casualties of battle. The lists of the dead and wounded of Partick parish weren't long, but Alice knew some names well. Charlie Morrison, a childhood friend of her brother-in-law Richard. Jim, the older brother of Caroline Ridley, whom she knew from Stewartville school. The son of Robert Ritchie, the local butcher who hadn't uttered a word since the telegram arrived. The healthy men of fighting age who weren't away were either excused from service or busy building war ships down on the docks. And if there was one type of man Alice was not interested in, it was a man who had anything to do with ships.

At times, when the very air of Partick parish felt thick with grief, Alice had allowed herself to wonder what use it was to sing. She found it difficult to reconcile the words of worship her choir sang for the god who had allowed this war to begin—and who had let it continue for years—with the beauty and symmetry of the melodies and harmonies that supported them. A musical work had a beginning, a middle and an end. But not this war.

On stage, though, Alice found it easy to imagine herself in a different time and place. Covent Garden. Royal Albert Hall. The Paris Opera. Instead of selected highlights, performing a full production of Theodora *to a musically knowledgeable and adoring audience. Despite Alice never having been someone's sweetheart, the role of Theodora, the Christian martyr and lover of Didymus, had become her signature.*

The respectful silence that dropped like a curtain when she opened her mouth was almost palpable. She imagined velvet draped around her, instead of the gown that she had sewn herself from a bolt of her former employer Mrs Rankin's cheapest silk. In the warmth of the

Windsor Halls spotlights, with the electric current running between her and the attentive bodies in their seats, while she sang passionately of love and enforced separations, it was easy for Alice to forget that she was twenty-two and had never left Glasgow.

17

If I'd known that Jane Austen had been a serious piano student as a teenager then perhaps I would have tried harder to enjoy *Emma*, which, to my profound irritation, was required reading for our final year of high school.

Although Austen was a much more accomplished musician than her creation Emma Woodhouse, she was not nearly as impressive at the keyboard as her most accomplished pianist, the enigmatic Jane Fairfax. Dedicated to her piano studies, Jane Fairfax was modest about her musicianship, and isolated by her beauty and talent. Though she always struck me as a significantly more intriguing character than Emma, in class I said nothing, by now superbly trained in the art of withholding a dissenting thought. In Virginia Woolf's first novel, *The Voyage Out*, the isolated but privileged Rachel Vinrace confesses her distaste for Jane Austen to a horrified Clarissa Dalloway: 'She's so—so—well, so like a tight plait.' I couldn't have agreed more. I held so many such thoughts that I felt it essential to share none of them. Listening to the incessant torrent of contrariness in my head made it all but impossible for me to hear anything else clearly.

I failed utterly to see what enchanted my peers about Emma Woodhouse. I thought she was a self-satisfied know-it-all, a spoiled daddy's girl held in undeserved high esteem by a tiny claustrophobic community, and who gets everything she wants. Blind to the parallels between my own privileged existence and that of Austen's heroine, I dismissed *Emma* as romantic pap. I choked on the limited options available to women in the first years of the nineteenth century, confused as to why we were reading about them in the latter decades of the twentieth.

Of all the things that bored me about the novel, what bothered me most was its obsession with marriage. The girls in my English class who had swooned over Mr Darcy in *Pride and Prejudice* the year before were now gaga about Mr Knightley. Why were sixteen- and seventeen-year-old girls in the late 1980s fantasising about marriage to a wealthy landowner, or to anyone? Marriage seemed to be the answer to almost any question the inhabitants of Austen's novels could think of.

I was enormously relieved to discover, years later, that Ralph Waldo Emerson shared my concerns about Austen's primary subject in his private notebook from the summer of 1861: 'Never was life so pinched & narrow. The one problem in the mind of the writer in both the stories I have read, "Persuasion", and "Pride & Prejudice", is marriageableness; all that interests any character introduced is still this one, has he or she money to marry with, & conditions conforming? . . . Suicide is more respectable.'

Outside my classroom, a ferocious pairing-off was taking place that had nothing at all to do with wedlock. At North Sydney train station, the girls' school girls looked at the boys' school boys looking at them. I would glance up from the novel I was reading to observe them through the windows of the bus, which I had ridden alone from Circular Quay in order to avoid social persecution. The girls boarded the bus squealing over seismic social developments that had just taken place on the train or the station platform, chewing gum to offset the cigarette smoke, their chins bright with pash-rash.

I couldn't wait to be rid of the lot of them. Looking down my nose at everybody else was a paltry substitute for self-esteem. I dreamed of the University of Sydney, where I imagined that interesting men who wanted to discuss books and music roamed the campus like bison on the prairie. Before that day came, I could fantasise about Vince Jones and his band of musical men.

I hurried down the steps to the Basement with my oldest friend, Daniela, hoping no one had observed us getting out of my father's car. We were sixteen going on twenty-three—or at least, that's how I liked to think of us. For some reason I regarded twenty-three as a magical age by which I would not only look my best but also have this growing-up thing all figured out and confidently be pursuing my highly successful adult life.

Because my father had dropped us off for tonight's gig, Daniela's dad would be picking us up. At 11 p.m. On a Sunday night. In the era before mobile phones, our suggested pick-up times were estimates at best. It took a few concerts before we understood that jazz clubs operated on a schedule that bore little relation to the advertised performance times, and none whatsoever to the needs of an overprotective parent.

We had come to the Basement to see Vince Jones: trumpet player, singer and composer. As teenagers, our musical tastes were more mature than the rest of us, as though we were baby giraffes whose long legs had to wait for the rest of their bodies to catch up. Admittedly, Daniela was the one with long legs; my emerging shape was closer to that of a double bass. Make that a cello.

It was so early in the evening that no one stood at the door collecting entry fees or looking out for horribly underage jazz fans. Once inside, we ordered Tia Marias with milk from bartenders who were kind enough not to laugh, and scoured the cosy venue for a seat with a view of the stage. Depending on how early we arrived at these gigs, we scored a bar stool each, one stool that we shared, or a dark corner of beer-stained carpet near the toilets, where we shifted our weight from one leg to the other while we waited up to two hours for the band to come on stage. When our Tia Maria budget was blown, we sipped water. Inside the Basement, H_2O existed only in pricey sealed plastic bottles like a harbinger of the environmental future.

Vince Jones came to Sydney every three months or so, bringing with him several musicians who looked to be in their twenties, plus an extraordinary pianist named Barney McAll who seemed hardly older than Daniela and me. *Fancy being so talented that you could leave school and travel around playing music like this*, I thought.

I can't remember how I first came to hear the music of Vince Jones. Born in Scotland, like my grandmother Alice, he emigrated with his parents to the mining town of Wollongong on the New South Wales coast in the mid-1960s, when he was eleven. Absorbing his father's jazz record collection, Jones attributes the beginning of his real interest in jazz to hearing *Sketches of Spain* when he was fourteen. The sound of Miles Davis inspired a working-class white boy to pick up a trumpet and start writing his own songs, a perfect example of D.H. Lawrence's idea of the 'blind reaching out for beauty'.

From this tough environment sprang a musician who wrote songs about protecting the environment, respect for women, and the nature of power. My ears had been drenched in jazz standards and the Top 40. The lyrics of the former are full of women treating their man wrong, men abandoning women, misery and loss. On commercial radio, all I heard were songs about sex, featuring banal rhymes: *Hold me tight / morning light / feel all right* and all that . . . jazz. The dominant number one singles in 1986 included 'Venus' by Bananarama, John Farnham's 'You're the Voice', Madonna's 'Papa Don't Preach', and the comic version of 'Living Doll' by The Young Ones with Cliff Richard. Jones's songs, originating from a profound sense of social justice, were a revelation.

I'd started to fantasise about one day writing books and plays. The marks my new English teacher gave me for my essays were so good that I felt for the first time that I could form an original opinion about a text and clearly express it on the page. Despite the increasing intensity of my piano studies—I was preparing for eighth grade, the final level of exams prior to the performance diploma—I really couldn't see any point in continuing to the Sydney Conservatorium of Music, which seemed the inevitable next step. Even if I was good enough, which I doubted, I already knew I didn't aspire to join an orchestra or teach. The only place I wanted to play the piano was on a stage like in the Basement, as part of a jazz ensemble. But I dismissed the idea as ludicrous: I'd never seen a woman pianist in a live jazz band, and there were no women pianists in the bands in my father's record collection.

♫

My mother never once encouraged me to aspire to marriage for its own sake. 'These days, when girls earn money and go where they please, I just don't know why you would,' she said repeatedly. Then, as an afterthought: 'Unless you wanted children, of course.' I think she had concluded from my limited childhood interest in dolls that I wasn't overly maternal.

In the mid-1980s, when my mother first began drip-feeding me what I heard as her preference that I remain single, my parents had been married for twenty-five years. In her words I hear ambivalence about the institution of which she remains a member—and the fact of her financial dependence on my father. I hear her saying that while it's nothing personal, if she had felt she'd had another choice to make, she might well have made it.

As a teenager I thought the point of our education was that we could make our way in the world independently of—or interdependently with—men. Reading *Emma*, I felt coerced into admiring Mr Knightley because he owned most of the surrounding land. As far as I could tell, all he'd done was inherit it—literally born lucky. Other male characters with admirable traits but fewer resources were passed over like barren ground. It infuriated me that a school whose supposed mission was to encourage young women to live fulfilling and independent lives was feeding us this diet of fantasy. That it was somehow acceptable, even encouraged, for a teenage girl to aim for a rich man rather than become independent. Reading about the social calibrations of bright young women thrown together because of proximity and socio-economics, at the expensive girls-only school my parents struggled to pay for, felt claustrophobic.

I failed to grasp the sexual politics of Austen's world: the inconvenient truth that in the early decades of the nineteenth century, marriage was the one chance any woman had of making a secure future for herself. Austen's portrait of small-town English life, her nuanced characterisations of unremarkable people, and her empathy with Emma's struggle to keep from meddling in other people's lives and to know her own flaws, passed over my sixteen-year-old head like the elements of the periodic table in Chemistry class.

My naive sympathies lay with the troubled heroines of Thomas Hardy's Wessex, a romantic fictional universe in which working-class women were admired from afar, then from close up, then left for dead, socially and financially speaking. In Hardy's novels, men often held the power to ruin a woman's life, but the passion between the characters seemed beautiful and painful and true. In reading, I could indulge my insatiable taste for melancholy, fascinated by the exquisite struggles of fictional others, because I'd not experienced anything like it and was quite certain I'd be clever enough to avoid that sort of thing.

♫

Emma Wedgwood was one of the more naturally talented of the many upper middle-class women studying the piano in Britain in the first decades of the nineteenth century. With a family fortune made in pottery, Emma, like so many of her contemporaries in fiction, was never in the market for an actual job. As a star piano student at the Greville House school, she performed for Prince George of Wales' consort Mrs Fitzherbert, studied with the virtuoso pianist Ignaz Moscheles, took several lessons with Chopin, and completed her grand tour of Europe when she was sixteen. By the age of thirty, Emma Wedgwood had had the economic luxury of declining several offers of marriage. When she accepted the proposal of her first cousin, the naturalist Charles Darwin, she understood her job was to propagate the species.

In his 1871 *Descent of Man, and Selection in Relation to Sex*, written more than thirty years after his marriage to Emma, Darwin argues that birdsong and human music are

the outcomes of the evolutionary process called sexual selection: 'The impassioned . . . musician, when with his varied tones and cadences he excites the strongest emotions in his hearers, little suspects that he uses the same means by which, at an extremely remote period, his half-human ancestors aroused each other's ardent passions, during their mutual courtship and rivalry.'[49]

Ardent passions indeed: following their wedding in January 1839, Emma Darwin was pregnant for more than a decade, bearing ten children, of whom seven survived. As this picture of domestic harmony suggests, music-making remained an important part of their marriage.

'The suspicion does not appear improbable that the progenitors of man, either the males or females, or both sexes, before they had acquired the power of expressing their mutual love in articulate language, endeavoured to charm each other with musical notes and rhythm,' Darwin concluded.[50]

One hundred and twenty years after Darwin published these words, such ancient charms were working on me through Vince Jones and his band. Our love wasn't mutual, but I didn't care. I parsed the lyrics of his original songs, looking for insights into the workings of his mind, imagining the day when we met and became—what? Friends? Colleagues? Lovers? Truly it was as ludicrous a fantasy as that entertained about marriage by the girls with whom I had studied *Emma*.

On reflection, I suspect what I responded to most strongly was the distinctiveness of Jones's own compositions and the unmistakeable sound of his voice. It was probably the first time I had experienced, regularly and up close, the extraordinary power of an original creative artist. It was his *voice*—not just in the sense of his distinctive singing style, but also of his unique approach to songwriting and interpreting familiar tunes by folk and soul singers—that so charmed me, in the Darwinian sense. I suppose that's what I wanted to be myself: original and distinctive in some way. Yet I felt as ordinary and invisible as everyone else, and too self-conscious to risk standing out.

The members of Vince Jones's band always wore suits. Perhaps it was because they were from Melbourne, where somehow I already understood that the men dressed with more care than their Sin City counterparts. But to be honest, I didn't care what they wore: their melodies and rhythms, as Darwin put it, were enough for me. Their clothes weren't for my benefit. If they were willing to don a suit, I reasoned, then it didn't seem beyond the realm of possibility that one day I could drag one of them home to meet my parents.

18

Petty Officer John Henry Edwards stood just over six feet tall in his Royal Navy uniform, his hat in one hand, a bottle of whisky for his host in the other. While on furlough with Alice's brother Vincent, Mr Edwards had endeared himself to the Taylors in two key respects. First, he had attended church on both Sundays since he and Vincent had been ashore. Second, he had recommended Vincent be reclassified on the Mameluke *from stoker second class—a filthy job that demanded the relentless shovelling of coal into the ship's boiler—to stoker first class, a promotion worth an extra five pence per day.*

Alice, who had heard about little else than Mr Edwards for the past two weeks, wasn't surprised to see him sitting at the dinner table when she returned from the Sunday service at Gardner Street. But she found herself disappointed. Mr Edwards was polite but distant, withholding the smile that had dazzled her when Vincent had introduced him after her Windsor Halls recital.

As the men discussed the intricacies of the Mameluke's *engineering, Alice wondered how much this effort at sociability was for the purpose of pairing them off. At first she had flattered herself to imagine that Vincent and her parents weren't-so-subtly trying to bring them together. But nothing in Mr Edwards' behaviour suggested he was here under false pretences. The* Mameluke *was in repairs for a few short weeks, and that was all. Once Alice had wrestled her unreasonable hopes into that logical straitjacket, she looked up and caught her mother's eye. Her left eyebrow was raised slightly in a gesture that managed to be both commentary and question about the stranger at their table. At least Alice was clear on her mother's agenda.*

'And where do you call home, Mr Edwards?' asked Charlotte Taylor during a pause in the men's conversation.

Alice observed Mr Edwards put down his knife and fork and wipe the corners of his mouth with his serviette, as if weighing how much he would share with his hosts. The air in the room, already heady with smoke from her father's pipe, thickened in the silence.

Then, his voice quiet, Mr Edwards began to speak of his wife Ann and their son Alistair. About how they had been married for several years before she became pregnant, and about how he had feared to go on active duty and leave her in Plymouth while she was yet to give birth. Around the table the Taylors listened to the story of the telegram that conveyed the news of Ann's haemorrhage giving birth to Alistair, who did not survive his mother.

'The Mameluke*'s my home, Mrs Taylor,' Mr Edwards said. 'I'm not ashamed to say I've even been glad of the war. Wouldn't have known what to do with myself otherwise.'*

When he stopped speaking, Mr Edwards looked hard at Alice for a moment, then lowered his eyes to his empty plate.

Vincent broke the silence. 'Had no idea, John,' he said. 'Bloody awful.'

Alice's father reached for his serviette and coughed for the sake of doing something. Her mother filled the awkward void with the sort of phrases Alice expected Mr Edwards had heard a thousand times.

'I am very sorry,' Alice added for want of what, she realised, she really wanted to say. That her empathy was as bottomless as the ocean for this man who had known loss of an order she could hardly fathom, and that she felt petty for the small aggravations she nurtured. She stood to clear the plates, not just because she felt more secure when she was in motion, but also because her action signalled to Mr Edwards that she believed that life unfolds in small moments like this one, and that feeling for another person—much like the revelation of a new piece of music—was a matter of gradual understanding and restraint. To be working as a choirmistress and performing regularly, with a home to return to and people to love—these things suddenly appeared precious and fragile to her.

Mr Edwards pushed back his chair and stood too. 'Please, Miss Taylor, let me help you,' he said.

19

In the humid confinement of the English Lit tutorial room, other first-year undergrads waxed lyrical about the Renaissance love poetry of Thomas Wyatt while I clung like mould to my vinyl chair. Our poodle-haired tutor smiled encouragement at his most frequent contributor, Jeremy, who needed no encouragement to start talking or, once he was underway, to continue.

'It's fascinating to imagine Wyatt writing these poems while travelling as an ambassador for Henry the Eighth,' Jeremy said. He must have been paying attention during the interminable lectures by the dour Professor Johnson, whose ghostly intonation could lull the worst insomniac into a restful nap.

Jeremy wasn't what I'd had in mind when I'd pictured the men I would meet on the University of Sydney campus. Although he was still a teenager, he dressed like a middle-aged academic in cardigans and spotless cream-coloured loafers. Not only had he read and understood every work set for tutorial discussion, but he had also conceived an opinion about it that he could express without hesitation in front of others. Jeremy spoke in complete sentences with the low volume and even tone of a guided meditation. His Shakespeare essay—composed entirely in iambic pentameter—had made him an instant star of the English department.

'Extraordinary, to think Wyatt was translating Petrarch and writing the first sonnets in English,' Jeremy said.

Extraordinary, I thought, *to be able to think of anything to contribute to the conversation.*

The tutor turned to the three or four of us who sat in stunned silence every week. 'Does anyone else have something to say about Wyatt?' The class understood his question to be rhetorical. I had nothing to share with the room but carbon dioxide.

Sitting in the tutorials or among hundreds of strangers in the cavernous lecture halls of the Wallace Theatre and the Merewether Building, I felt as useless and invisible as the first-year Arts student that I was. Considering myself a refugee from high school, I had assumed I was immigrating to a country where I at least spoke the language. I hadn't anticipated an environment in which I would feel perpetually stupid, and have nothing to say and no language in which to articulate it. I had no lofty professional goal, no specific social justice cause burning inside my middle-class breast. All I had brought with me to classes was a generic passionate intensity and a fantasy about writing books and plays.

I was still studying the piano and working toward my diploma—the culmination of all those years of exams at the Sydney Conservatorium of Music. I had locked myself to the piano stool for years, the key in my own hand. Now, aimlessly drifting about the campus, I was no longer chained to the instrument but still preferred not to stray far from it.

In Anton Chekhov's 1898 story 'Ionitch', pianist Ekaterina Ivanovna meets up with her former suitor on her return to her home village after years of intensive training at the Moscow Conservatory. Ekaterina, whose nickname is Kitten, had rejected Ionitch's marriage proposal because she loved music 'frantically' and wanted to be an artist. Back home again, she is more circumspect. 'I was such a queer girl then,' she confesses to Ionitch, who has long stopped thinking of her. 'I imagined myself such a great pianist. Nowadays all young ladies play the piano, and I played, too, like everybody else, and there was nothing special about me.'

On the university campus, the specialist knowledge I'd gained through twelve years of serious piano study was redundant. I was like Ekaterina returning to her village, only in my case the village was neither a familiar environment nor the utopia I had impatiently craved throughout high school. When Ekaterina arrives in her village she discovers, like many a passionate traveller has done, that while she may have changed, everything else has not. My experience was the opposite of Kitten's: I hadn't changed at all, I had in fact gone nowhere, yet everything around me was different, foreign, frightening. Away from my piano, I was a useless nobody, aimless as the lost Kitten.

♫

When a job came up at Mrs Dalton's ballet school in Hunters Hill, I leapt. It was at this school, although inside a different church hall, that I had fumbled a year's worth of jazz ballet steps as an uncoordinated six-year-old. Twelve years later, like Kitten returning to her Russian village, I was going back to dance classes—minus the leotard. Everything else remained unchanged. The elegant and reed-thin Mrs Dalton, who had struck fear into my tubby torso, was still teaching, still elegant, and only marginally less thin.

Twice a week for three hours I accompanied classes of girls while they learned to plié and pirouette, a dream part-time job that required no preparation. On campus I might have been clueless about Renaissance poetry, but I could still play a new piece at first sight. All I had to do was quickly identify appropriate music from the books piled on the battered upright, according to Mrs Dalton's instruction.

A piece with a rhythmic pattern that answered the call for 'skipping music', for example, or passages of semiquavers that met the brief for 'running music', or lots of staccato so that my fingers leapt off the keys just like the dancers' slippered feet during 'jumping music'. At the end of each class, the youngest girls, lined up in rows of pink tutus and white legs like oversize packets of marshmallows, thanked 'Miss Virginia' in singsong unison. Inside the ballet school I was happy because I felt useful.

As my shift wore on into the early evening and the girls grew taller and older, I couldn't deny the physical benefits that years of ballet lessons and home-based practice had effected in their adolescent bodies. Looking at the fourteen- and fifteen-year-old swans from the corner of my eye, I could see that their training had literally shaped the young women they would become. All those countless exercises and repetition to drill technique into their minds and muscles would influence both the shape of their thighs and their capacity to do the work required to reach any goal they set themselves.

Despite my serious piano study, I had developed a strong aversion to repetition as a way of rejecting the routines of my own childhood. Now I saw that repetition—the self-discipline and satisfaction accrued in days, weeks, months and years of activity and practice—could be, in and of itself, honourable. I had interpreted Mrs Dalton's self-presentation as a passive resistance to change—she still wore her straight grey hair in the same severe style, blunt cut at her collar-bone, and she still stood at the front of her classes in third position—but suddenly I saw her, solid and implacable, as part of a continuum of knowledge. Her life had been shaped by ballet, and she had chosen to pass on her expertise to generations of future dancers. Teaching was a manifestation of personal value, and repetition its necessary and active expression. This was as true at the barre as it was at the piano, on the tennis court, in my father's fundraising efforts and even in my mother's domestic routines.

As a pianist, I had reached an uncommon level of proficiency, and yet I had dismissed my achievement as being without value. There *was* value in providing accompaniment to the dancers—and the proof of it was that Mrs Dalton paid me for the service. There was value in playing with others, too, but aside from this ballet school job, I had sequestered my musicianship into rigorous private practice and study for my final examination: the gruelling performance diploma, called the Associate of Music Australia.

During lessons with Mr McFarlane I had begun hearing more frequently about the virtuosic feats of his star pupil, Jonathan Holmes. Now it appeared that nineteen-year-old Jonathan, a year older than I, was preparing for his debut concerto with a local amateur orchestra. 'Perhaps next year you'll be ready for that,' my teacher suggested one afternoon as we hunched over Chopin's *Revolutionary Study.* The staves snapped back into focus like the bars of a cage. I had been daydreaming—and not of playing with an orchestra.

If I'd thought about it seriously, I would have noticed that, outside the extreme demands of the world of classical music, thousands of musicians forged satisfying careers without reaching the level of technical dexterity I had. The most important thing for a musician is having your own voice, your own approach, and sounding like no one else. Guided by my punitive self-talk, by an upbringing that emphasised a pay cheque over creative play, and by my very limited understanding, a life in music just never seemed a possible course of action for me.

20

As Alice walked towards the altar of Dowanhill United Free Church on 5 September 1917, in the same pale-grey dress she had worn to sing at Windsor Halls just weeks earlier, she didn't mind that the wedding she'd never expected to have had been so hastily arranged. Nor was she troubled by the fact that some of those who had known her the longest appeared to have difficulty in feeling genuinely happy for her. As she walked up the aisle on her father's arm, wearing her grandmother's pearl earrings and matching choker, all she could see was John Henry Edwards. There he waited, the buttons of his uniform winking as he grinned with pride and anticipation.

Standing beside the man who would soon be her husband, Alice sensed her own life beginning to blossom at last. She would have time alone with John and discover all the secrets of a honeymoon, before he rejoined the Mameluke *next week. Alice's blood surged in her veins. She had never known such impatience before, or this longing for things she did not yet understand. She did not doubt that John would return safely to her. But for now, Alice's wait was over.*

When Mrs Edwards sang solo on the first Sunday after John sailed back to the North Sea, not one parishioner among the two congregations who heard her wasn't moved by the power and devotion in her voice. Alice herself was shocked at the sound she produced. It was as if a secret chamber of emotion had suddenly unlocked, unleashing a depth of feeling that no one, not even the soloist, had imagined had lain dormant inside her modest upright frame.

21

In April 1822, when Luigi Cherubini began work as the new director of the Conservatoire de Paris—then the most esteemed institution of music study in the world—he was shocked to discover there were forty-one women and thirty-two men in the piano performance stream, a combined total that far outweighed students for any other instrument. Cherubini declared the abundance of aspiring virtuosi '*abusive et pernicieuse*' and enforced a balance of fifteen men and fifteen women.[51] Despite his best efforts, women continued to dominate piano studies in many conservatories during the nineteenth century, though for many women this was a professional dead end.

Women weren't permitted to join professional orchestras, and Clara Schumann's public performances were the exception that proved the rule that women concert pianists had almost no career prospects. Nor did specialised training guarantee a woman pianist that she would be a good piano teacher, or that she would be paid well enough to support herself.[52] The nineteenth-century piano virtuosa was the terrible progeny of Dr Frankenstein's monster: a previously unimaginable creature with extraordinary powers, for which there was no corresponding social function.

In his *Letters to a Young Lady*, his ideal piano student, Czerny makes no reference to the idea of her teaching. Nor does he mention solo performance, accompanying, or any other method by which Cecilia could earn income. Czerny assumes that Cecilia has a stable home while she secures her financial future; the art of playing the pianoforte was for domestic cultivation and enjoyment only. Czerny could compose and teach, and perform in public, but not Cecilia—her skills were only ever to be employed indirectly in the securing of income. They would serve as the amuses-bouche to the main meal: finding a suitable man to marry.

Musical women without the financial security of a family or a husband were in a much more precarious social and economic position. The one respectable profession available to an unmarried woman was to become a governess. The stories of other fictional nineteenth-century women, such as the orphans Jane Fairfax and Jane Eyre, and Miles Franklin's Sybella Melvin at the turn of the twentieth, demonstrate how piano skills formed a crucial part of a young woman's economic value as a governess.

In *Emma*, before Jane Fairfax's secret engagement to Frank Churchill is revealed, she is destined to become a governess. In this exchange between Jane and Mrs Churchill about finding a suitable position, Austen makes clear her thoughts on the subject: "'I did not mean,' replied Jane, "I was not thinking of the slave-trade; governess-trade, I assure you, was all that I had in view; widely different certainly as to the guilt of those who carry it on; but as to the greater misery of the victims, I do not know where it lies.'"

The heroine of Charlotte Brontë's *Jane Eyre* (1847, though set earlier in the nineteenth century) has only a basic competence at the keyboard, but this is combined with her French language skills, her embroidery and her minor works on canvas. Her accomplishments paint her, in the words of her former nurse Bessie, as 'quite a lady'. If Jane were a real lady of her era, she wouldn't need to travel alone to Thornfield Hall to teach Mr Rochester's ward Adèle in exchange for a roof over her head. Having come to hope that she might be the object of Mr Rochester's affection, Jane learns the painful news of her employer's visit to the Leas estate, where—according to the housekeeper Mrs Fairfax—he sang duets with the beautiful heiress Blanche Ingram. In order to sober up, Jane forces herself to imagine drawing a chalk likeness of what she sees in the mirror. 'A more fantastic idiot had never surfeited herself on sweet lies,' she concludes of herself, before setting to work on two portraits: one based on the reported loveliness of Miss Ingram, the other an unvarnished self-portrait in crayon. She titles the latter *Portrait of a Governess, disconnected, poor, and plain.*

Charlotte Brontë dedicated *Jane Eyre* to William Thackeray, whose heroine Becky Sharp, another orphan, makes a giant leap forward for women at the piano by tearing off her velvet gloves. 'Give me money, and I will teach them,' declares Becky to Miss Pinkerton in *Vanity Fair* (1848). In one sentence the enterprising Becky announces herself to be a woman of high ambition and low social standing. In having her teach the aristocratic young ladies among whom she is billeted at Miss Pinkerton's Academy, the headmistress is hoping to save money. Becky's classmates and teachers cringe at her insistence on being paid, but she doesn't think twice about using her piano skills to earn money, and in so doing to assert her financial independence. In this respect, Becky Sharp is an important figure in the genealogy of piano-playing literary heroines: she's the first to reject the servitude of being a governess and embrace her ability to provide a service with economic value.

As a teenager I never understood why becoming a governess was such a terrible misfortune. You could read, write, play the piano and have a secure roof over your head. Jane Eyre was settling in pretty comfortably until she fell in love with her boss. But without choice, the life of a governess is one of vulnerability and shame—most vividly demonstrated in *My Brilliant Career*, in which Sybella Melvin is forced to become governess to the eight children of Peter M'Swat in order to pay off a debt her father incurred.

Many real musical women across Europe enacted the same small-scale tragedy of market forces suffered by Chekhov's fictional Ekaterina Ivanovna. The laws of supply and demand applied equally in the concert halls of Vienna and Paris as they did in the small towns of Russia. In the 1881 British Census, 26,000 people counted themselves among the category of 'Musicians and Music Masters'. The 1911 census records more than 47,000 in the same category.[53] Any freelancer can understand the implications.

At the beginning of the nineteenth century, Jane Austen's heroines played the piano while waiting for marriage proposals. By the end of it, when Ekaterina resigns herself to becoming a governess, piano teaching had become a respectable profession for unmarried women. In fact, teaching was the only opportunity available to the dozens of musically gifted women returning home from years of dedicated study on the Continent. The figure of the spinster piano teacher or governess was perhaps a little to be pitied, though far from rare. The invention and mass production of the piano had led, like all technologies do, to unintended consequences. Those who didn't nab a husband looked to teaching to earn an income while remaining respectable. Kitten and her cohort found themselves valued at a dime a dozen. The excess supply of talented women created a new musical underclass: the overeducated private piano teacher.

22

'Hello, Richard, come on in,' I said to the head of fair hair bent over his satchel at my front door. He gripped the leather bag to his chest as if it were a Homeric shield. I couldn't imagine what he carried inside it. To get to my house, he had only to descend the driveway from his own home, which perched on the steep hill on the north side of sleepy George Street, and cross to its south side. An odyssey of less than one minute.

'Hello,' Richard mumbled, his eyes darting in every direction except my face. He stood with his shoulders hunched, as if expecting someone more important to sneak up behind him at any minute. My first task would be trying to get him to relax. I closed the door behind him and set off up the stairs to the piano room, which was still Sitting Quietly after all these years.

Richard looked so grown up. Though it had been two or three years since I had been this close to him in person, we'd been neighbours all our lives. Most of our recent communication had been conducted in sedan semaphore, hands waving inside the windows of passing cars. He was taller than I'd expected: I was used to seeing him sitting inside a car rather than standing up, and he was only thirteen. Even so, he already dressed like a suburban dad. His sports jacket was ubiquitous among men who looked as though their only relation to physical activity had been to observe it from distant sidelines—men like his father, one of the wealthiest property developers in Sydney. I was unsure whether our mothers' agreement that I would teach Richard in half-hour increments once a week reflected my mother's marketing chops, his mother's faith in my untested teaching ability, or the serendipitous intersection of frugality and geographical convenience.

Although I had drawn the obvious conclusion that teaching beginners from the comfort of my home was better than any other part-time paying job I could get, Richard was my first student. Like my father, I had a knack for mining endless seams of volunteer work. During high school there had been my work experience stints at two different radio stations and one local newspaper. During the first year of my degree, in the fullest phase of my anxiousness to be useful in the world, I rose willingly at four in the morning in order to drive to the headquarters of a community radio station, where I paraphrased items from the local paper and read them on air every half an hour between 5 and 9 a.m. I had scored this dubious work experience myself. Among my father's Rotary coterie there were no contacts in the world of magazines and newspapers, where I sometimes fancied myself a budding Lois Lane.

My mobility at that moonlit hour had been due to my parents' generous gift of a second-hand Nissan Pulsar hatchback. Having to pay for my own petrol, insurance and registration was a key factor in my capitulation to the idea of teaching beginners. So was my mother's insistence that

I pay her a weekly *board* now that I had left school. She was unapologetic in viewing my continuing to live under *her roof*, as she had begun referring to the house I'd grown up in, as an economic transaction. Like the women in the novels I was reading, my mother did not generate an income. Despite advocating my financial independence, she never seemed concerned that she depended entirely on the man she married, as Earth does the sun. The economic exchange they had entered upon marriage was the crucial but invisible element of their ecosystem, rather like oxygen to the survival of the species. My mother's insistence on my financial contribution to the household—which I thought fair enough—meant I'd have to rustle up a few piano students. That wouldn't mean that I was, you know, becoming a piano teacher.

Richard slumped at the piano stool and looked directly ahead, as if waiting for take-off. I sat down behind him and to his right like a copilot. It then occurred to me that I had placed my chair in relation to the piano exactly where Mr McFarlane used to sit in relation to me. It was uncanny to be sitting in the teacher's seat, watching someone else—my student, no less—play my own piano. Instead of a mirror, it was like a window on an earlier self.

It was difficult to believe that Mr McFarlane made a satisfying life's work out of staring at the backs of adolescents, and unimaginable that my stint as a teacher was anything other than temporary. I hadn't a clue about what I'd eventually do for a living, but the thought of repeating myself was intolerable. Despite my observations of Mrs Dalton's older ballet students, the idea of doing the same thing year in year out—which is how I thought about everything from gaining a Law degree to raising children—still induced paralysis. If I chose not to think about the future, then it might just fail to show up.

'It might be a bit easier for you to play if you sat up straight, Richard.'

He pulled himself upright but kept his hands hanging at his sides like levers waiting to be pulled.

'Now, take your right hand and press this note here with your thumb.'

Richard touched the white note gently, as if it might set off an alarm.

'Do you see how that note is in the middle of the keyboard? We call that note Middle C.'

He remained silent.

'Try placing your second finger on the note to the right of Middle C—yes, good—and your third finger on the note to its right. Great!'

Richard stretched his fingers over the notes so tautly that the tips were almost raised off the tarmac, but it didn't matter. First contact had been made. The correct hand position would come. The piano police would have admonished me for this introduction of hand to keyboard, but Richard was at least five years too old for any passionate dedication to the instrument to stick.

I experienced a surprising sense of dominion over my student. As the piano teacher I assumed a position of authority that I felt I hadn't earned but would savour anyway. At least I was earning money. For an eighteen-year-old my habits were expensive, though I didn't buy illegal drugs or even cigarettes. After my car expenses, my spare change went on live performances by Vince Jones, special-import jazz CDs, and a subscription to *The New Yorker.* Each issue arrived by boat several weeks after publication, reinforcing my conviction that life was taking place elsewhere, a party to which I not only hadn't been invited, but which was over before I'd even heard about it. The magazines piled up on the carpet by my bed in a bonsai skyscraper as I dreamed of real ones: the Chrysler Building and Empire State.

Richard pressed Middle C again and kept his hand hovering over it while the sound died.

'Just like the alphabet has letters, the piano has notes,' I said. 'There are seven notes that repeat at different pitches, or levels, up and down the keyboard.'

Richard said nothing, but bent forward over his hand. It was amazing how he just sat there, listening to everything I said. The authority was intoxicating.

'I think you're a little close to the piano, Richard. Try moving the seat back a bit. And remember to sit up str—'

He raised his hands as if to grab the edge of the piano stool, then they paused midair and shivered. At first I took this for an expression of rebellion, a refusal to accept either the form or the content of my instruction. But I concluded it was anxiety—I'd had no idea he would be so nervous.

'Richard, are you all right?'

He gave no response, but jerked his head in a precise flicking motion a lawn-watering system might make. I leaned forward to catch his eye, but he was somewhere else. Wherever he had gone, there was no music.

Prior to the lesson, Richard's mother had explained they were trialling new epilepsy medication that could have the paradoxical side effect of increasing the frequency of his seizures. Behind his twitching head I glanced at my watch. The lesson was fast disappearing. I had taught him nothing.

Richard cradled his head in his hands. 'Sorry,' he muttered.

I let out the breath I'd been holding for the duration of his epileptic fit, somewhere between twenty seconds and two minutes. 'Are you okay?' I asked again, for something to say. Thankfully he nodded, keeping his head down as if he wished he could plunge nose-first into the shag pile.

When Richard politely declined my offer of a glass of water, I decided to proceed as if every student had a seizure during a lesson with me. I got up from my chair and propped open a beginner's book on the piano's music shelf. It seemed too much for me to ask Richard's brain to process new information, but I didn't know what else to do. He looked up.

'Have you seen music written down before?' I asked.

He shook his head. I worried the action might trigger another fit, but the electrical storm in his head seemed to have passed. The rest of his body was eerily still.

'Well, this is what it looks like,' I continued. 'These five black lines, we call that a stave.'

'Why?' he said, not moving a muscle. I couldn't tell whether his rigidity was from fear of prompting another seizure, or sheer anxiety.

'I'm not sure,' I admitted. 'That's just what it's called. The notes you play correspond to the black circles on or between the lines. For example, the bottom line on this stave is E, here,' I said, pressing the note above Middle C. I had gotten ahead of myself, and way ahead of any beginner's first lesson, let alone someone who had just experienced a seizure. But in a kind of immunisation theory of teaching the instrument, I believed Richard deserved maximum value for his minimal exposure to the piano.

Richard shifted in his seat and frowned. 'But why?' he said.

'What do you mean?'

'Who says that line means E?'

I was stumped. Not once had it occurred to me to question the basis of Western music notation.

'Well, this system came into use hundreds of years ago,' I began, struggling for an answer. Now I felt like a chump for never having wondered about it myself.

'But why should it?'

If I were a better teacher—or any kind of teacher, really—I would have anticipated my student's resistance and prepared a response to it. And I don't know if anyone can learn anything while being under fire from one's own brain. But Richard had started to irritate me.

How could I explain that we were stuck with the five-line staves as much as we were with the alphabet? Nothing can be altered in the 'notation of music by dead masters', Elfriede Jelinek wrote in her 1983 novel *Die Klavierspielerin,* which appeared in English five years later as *The Piano Teacher.* Her protagonist Erika Kohut, a failed concert performer, has shifted like the translated title from player to teacher, scaring the bejesus out of most of her students. Part of me wanted to believe Richard's inference that an alternative system of notation might be possible. Who was I to dismiss the idea? I had learned the system in the traditional way and swallowed its prescriptions like medicine—reading black and white marks on staves of black lines, connecting them to the black and white notes on the keyboard. Now I was perpetuating the transfer of knowledge by teaching it without question to my own student. But Erika Kohut—living with her mother, tormented by sadomasochism and her artistic failure—is trapped by more than the notes:

> Erika has been harnessed in this notation system since earliest childhood. Those five lines have been controlling her ever since she first began to think. She mustn't think of anything but those five black lines. This grid system, together with her mother, has hamstrung her in an untearable net of directions, directives, precise commandments, like a rosy ham on a butcher's hook. This provides security, and

> security creates fear of uncertainty. Erika is afraid that everything will remain as it is, and she is afraid that someday something could change.

Fearful of change, and terrified of things staying the same: that was me all over.

I looked at Richard. 'Do you have an idea for how else we could notate music?' I said. I wasn't being facetious—part of me wondered if he had something of what was then called the *idiot savant* about him. Perhaps the peculiar wiring of his brain facilitated musical insights unavailable to those of us limited by more conventional neural pathways. If anyone could devise an alternative system, maybe it was him.

'Not yet,' he said, with no trace of irony.

Before I could embarrass myself further, Richard had two mini-fits in quick succession. 'Let's leave it for today,' I said when he came to, relieved for an excuse to conclude the lesson.

I sent him back across the street with two pieces of homework: the first, to spend five minutes each day placing his right thumb on Middle C and stepping higher, note by note, using each finger of the right hand so as to familiarise himself with C, D, E, F and G; the second, to devise a new system of music notation. From behind the glass-panelled front door I watched him trudge up our short driveway to street level, cross the street and lean into the much steeper incline of the driveway to his home, which towered over ours. I'm not sure how his head felt, but mine was spinning.

Glancing out the kitchen window a few days later, I was astonished to spy Moby Dick through the floor-to-ceiling glass of Richard's living room window. An enormous white grand piano sat becalmed on what I knew to be an ocean of thick pea-green carpet, its gleaming lid open in full sail. I had worried that Richard's first lesson with me would also prove to be his last. Now, witnessing his parents' extravagance, I knew my fears were unfounded.

I would never be a piano teacher.

23

ALICE'S LETTER FROM THE ADMIRALTY OFFICE, dated 5 March 1918, was exactly six months after her wedding. The letter informed Alice that her application for the Navy Separation Allowance had been rejected. The allowance consisted of a portion of a soldier's pay, matched by the government, to provide for the dependents of those on active duty.

It's not clear to me when Alice submitted her application. The Christmas season is hectic for a choirmistress in any year, but in late 1917 Alice would have had to rehearse two concert programs with choral parts she amended herself to counteract the imbalance in her two choirs. With the war still raging, she would have been missing—for a second year—most of her tenors, and was probably too heavy in the bass section, with more older men filling in the gaps of the younger ones away in service. Perhaps Alice waited until the new year to apply. Perhaps she hoped that she wouldn't need it by then.

The letter declining her application, part of a bundle of correspondence my aunt Charlotte has kept for decades, contained an explanation, but it made no sense.

Madam,

With reference to your application for the grant of Navy separation allowance in respect of John Henry Edwards, Stoker Petty Officer 305849, I have to inform you that as it is reported that the man was already married and had a wife living when he went through a form of marriage with you in September last, it is regretted that you are not eligible for an allowance.

Your Certificate of Marriage is returned herewith.

Alice knew he'd been married. John had sat across from her at dinner and told her whole family the story. Ann had died in childbirth. The letter's wording was ugly, but clearly there had been an administrative error.

James Taylor determined to get to the bottom of this bureaucratic puzzle for his daughter's sake. Having expected that Alice would soon no longer represent a financial burden to him, James must have been outraged both for moral and financial reasons, and impatient for an answer. He sought the advice of George Bradley, a local solicitor.

The next six months unfolded between the pages of Mr Bradley's correspondence with the Admiralty. At first, the office would provide no new information regarding their decision to decline Alice's claim for support. They repeated their policy of not divulging additional details.

Admiralty,
10th July 1918

Sir/

In reply to your letter of the 15th ultimo, relative to the wife of John Henry Edwards, Stoker, Petty Officer, 305849,

I have to inform you that it is regretted that the information asked for cannot be furnished.

I have to add that all the circumstances were fully investigated in connection with the claim to Navy Separation Allowance received from this Petty Officer's present Allottee, and that the Department is satisfied that the facts are as represented in the letter addressed to her on the 5th March last.

I am, Sir,
Your obedient Servant,
(sgd) Frank Porter,
pr Accountant-General of the Navy.

But Mr Bradley, who would not take no for an answer, wrote again to the Admiralty. This time he set out in greater detail the circumstances in which Alice May Morrison Edwards, née Taylor, found herself in the summer of 1918.

Let's put ourselves in Alice's shoes as she greets John Henry Edwards, the man she married last September at the church she grew up in, as he returns to Glasgow for a conjugal visit. It's not clear exactly when he arrived, though from the correspondence I conclude it must have been in early summer. Did she greet him at the docks, or wait impatiently at home? Had she dreamed of being alone with her husband again, in whatever version of privacy the newlyweds—who until now had only spent a handful of days together—could muster? Perhaps she was torn between excitement, anticipation and an anxious knot in her stomach. On seeing his new wife again, did John lift Alice in his arms? Hug her with his whole body? Or greet her awkwardly, like the almost-stranger that she was? Even if Alice briefly regretted marrying him so soon after meeting him, I suspect, on seeing him again, she felt immediately reassured by his presence.

We don't know what, if anything, John knew about the Admiralty Office's decision before coming ashore. We don't know what Alice's mother made of the letter, though it's easy enough to imagine her being horrified at the mere hint of impropriety in relation to her daughter, even if it would turn out to be a simple clerical error. We will never know just how awkward the reunion was.

As expected, John Henry Edwards gave his wife and his in-laws a perfectly reasonable explanation for the mix-up. The 'present Allottee' of his Navy Separation Allowance was his dear mother. The mistake had all been his, in not informing the Admiralty of the change in his marital status. He apologised to Alice, James and Charlotte, reassuring them that he would sort everything out.

Did they believe him?

Would you?

As John was on a brief shore leave, he was desperate to be with his new wife. And, despite the bureaucratic bungle, she with him, I imagine. But I find it difficult to see Alice taking her husband upstairs to her bed while her parents were in the house. Perhaps Charlotte and James Taylor begrudgingly gave the newlyweds some time alone, and spent an afternoon staring into their drinks, thinking all the thoughts they dared not say out loud. Or they gave John the benefit of the doubt because they knew his history and it made sense that he'd been sending money to his mother after he had been widowed. Or they were riddled with doubt but from neither a legal nor moral standpoint could do anything about it, until Mr Bradley could pressure the Admiralty for an answer.

In early July, John Henry Edwards went back to sea aboard the *Mameluke*. On 10 July, a letter arrived from the Admiralty. Again their office refused to supply further information. One week later, Mr Bradley composed the following letter in response. It paints a vivid picture of the anxiety and despair now gripping the household at 370 Dumbarton Road.

102 Bath Street,
Glasgow, 18th July 1918
The Accountant General of the navy, Admiralty,
4a Newgate Street,
London, E. C. 1

Sir,

I duly received your reply dated 10th inst. to my letter to you of 15th ultimo, relative to the wife of John Henry Edwards,

Stoker Petty Officer, 305849, and your refusal to supply information asked.

I must ask you for your authority for withholding information. My client who supposes herself to be the wife of this man is at present in a terrible position, as since I wrote you John Henry Edwards has been living with her during a short leave, after persuading my client and his daughter that it was his mother who was getting the allowance. My client and his daughter are respectable citizens of this country and should it be the case that the Department is satisfied with the facts, as represented in the letter addressed by you to the lady on 5th March last, she must at once be put in possession of the necessary details to release her from the intolerable position in which she finds herself.

All I require from you is the name and address of the present allottee. I shall make all other necessary enquiries myself. I cannot conceive why you should conceal the name of the present allottee from a woman, who if your history be well founded, is the victim of a thorough paced scoundrel.

I am, Sir,
Your obedient Servant,
(sgd) George Bradley

But not a word of correspondence, no fresh scrap of information, arrived for the next two and a half months. Not one step was taken nearer to resolving what had by now surely become a torment to Alice. Mr Bradley refers to her 'intolerable position' and the possibility of Henry being a 'thorough paced scoundrel', but we have no way of knowing if these descriptions are Alice's. I doubt it; they sound much more like the words of her father and family solicitor, older men with a cynical suspicion of what the truth might be.

Mr Bradley followed up with the Admiralty on 4 September, the day before Alice's first wedding anniversary, with another inquiry, given that so much time had elapsed without response.

Finally, in the first week of October, Alice got her answer.

Admiralty,
5th October 1918

Sir,

With reference to your letter of the 4th ultimo, and previous correspondence, relative to the wife of John H. Edwards, Stoker Petty Officer, 305849, I have to inform you that the question of withholding the information asked for by you has been re-considered, and, in the special circumstances, it has been decided to make an exception to the general rule in this case.

I have accordingly to inform you that this Petty Officer was married in the Parish Church of Falmouth on the 13th September 1906 to Ann Barrett, and that, in February last, the latter was living at No. 2, Pembroke Lane, Devonport.

I am, Sir,
Your obedient Servant,
(sgd) C. M. Muir,
for Accountant-General of the Navy.

Her husband was still married to Ann. She had not died giving birth to their baby son. She was living in their home on the Royal Navy base in the south of England, carrying on the unpaid labour of child-rearing, while John Henry Edwards enjoyed shore leave and—after a hasty wedding to satisfy appearances in Glasgow—the affections of his shipmate's sister.

Alice reverted to her maiden name, though now it reverberated, if only between her own ears, with her humiliation of being neither married nor a maiden. Alice May Morrison Taylor fulfilled all the non-technical requirements of a spinster. Soon the people of Partick looked at her as they always had, with a mixture of respect and pity. The novelty of her having married a bigamist faded into the fabric of town life like a stain on carpet.

Yet how did Alice perceive herself? Double standards being what they are, I'm guessing her parents—perhaps in spite of efforts to avoid talking about it—made her feel like soiled goods, as though she would never appeal to any man now that she was no longer a virgin. What did the parishioners say about her? The members of her choirs? The neighbours? Perhaps they said nothing, and their silence roared in her ears as self-recrimination.

Or maybe Alice rejected their unspoken judgement, and felt furious that John's lies—so many lies!—had damaged her reputation while he sailed clear away.

24

On campus my love of contemporary jazz had all the social appeal of a cold sore. At the mention of jazz most people would stare at me, assume I was joking, and change the topic. 'Doesn't it all sound the same?' asked one boy, who was obsessed with heavy metal, without irony.

In Sydney the word *jazz* conjured images of banjos and clarinets, white-suited horn players lifting their instruments in tandem from the seated front row of a big band. Somehow in the Australian popular imagination, jazz had become untethered from its African-American roots, cast off from its history of expressing the yearning for liberation from oppression. The recordings of John Coltrane and Dizzy Gillespie and Roy Haynes and Betty Carter that I listened to sounded nothing like the music I heard live every week, but nor did I expect it to. The gigs I heard were largely played by middle-class boys. White boys who longed to express themselves outside the rigid confines of rock and pop—and who'd grown up in a country that provided health insurance. While they might struggle to get a girlfriend and pay the rent, they had always been free.

On campus I wanted desperately to excel, but my English Lit essay results, like me, were unremarkable. An adolescence spent reading books and studying the piano had made me as useful for any real-world application as the pianists in the novels I had read. My anxiety at feeling out of my depth and my mediocre results sent me scurrying into hiding. I was too shy to ask for help, too afraid to turn up for an audition at the dramatic society or to volunteer for the Arts Revue, too self-conscious to become a member of the tennis club. I didn't think that perhaps I had chosen the wrong subjects, or that possibly I wasn't ready for university. Nor did I imagine that anyone else felt as stupid, shy and awkward as I did. I had long fantasised about meeting new people, but up close they terrified me. They might discover that nothing was going on beneath my polished surface, that the still waters I presented were in fact pretty shallow.

Instead I haunted the gloomy research stacks of Fisher Library; the grey metal shelves carried the burden of all the literary ghosts whose works rested there in peace. I clutched a paper scribbled with author surnames and Dewey decimal numbers like a scrap of hieroglyph, but I didn't know what I was looking for. I had imagined my future would unfold like a pristine map, easy to read and the right way up at all times. I'd been wrong.

In that first year of university, I had a much better time off campus than on, reading books, studying for my piano performance diploma, working my volunteer and my three paid jobs. I spent my leisure time watching jazz musicians transcend self-consciousness to express themselves in public. During the late 1980s and early 1990s, the contemporary jazz scene in Sydney consisted of dozens of bands, around twenty-five musicians, and about five venues. In addition to the Basement, my live music orbit took in the Harbourside

Brasserie on the western side of the Harbour Bridge, the brightly lit Real Ale Cafe on King Street, the underground bunker of the Soup Plus Cafe on George, and the velvet darkness of Round Midnight in Kings Cross. Finding this live jazz netherworld was like stepping through the back of the wardrobe in C.S. Lewis's *Chronicles of Narnia*.

Daniela and I now sipped gin and tonics. Between songs and sets, we enjoyed listening to other people's conversations. One woman might complain to her friend, 'It doesn't sound the same as it does on the record,' and Daniela and I would turn to each other and smile into our drinks. That's the point—it's called *improvisation*. The sly attentions of men we caught looking at us also made us laugh. In fact, we laughed about as much as we could. It staved off the anxiety.

There were almost no women jazz musicians. Why was that? They seemed to be everywhere in other styles of music, fronting rock bands, strumming guitars, singing backup. Had there been one woman in any of the jazz bands I saw during my late teens and early twenties, I would have gone up to her during a break between sets and asked her how she did it. How did she fight through the muck of self-consciousness to play to the best of her ability in public? Did she feel self-doubt and go ahead anyway? Did she have a secret trick to drown out all the self-criticism in her head as she played? Did she believe other people when they told her she sounded great? Why didn't I?

Just as it had when I saw my first jazz concert at the age of six, live musical performance still seemed to be the best way to spend my time. But I was hung up on the dilemma of perfectionism. 'To be a professional musician one must be schizophrenic, with a split mind, half of which knows it is impossible to play perfectly, while the other half believes that to play perfectly is only a matter of time and devotion,' wrote Rebecca West in her posthumously published 1984 novel *This Real Night*, about budding concert pianist Rose Aubrey. Though West was writing of her heroine performing the classical repertoire, the principle was the same in a jazz setting. Unfortunately my mind was locked on the impossibility of perfection, convinced that no amount of time or devotion could help me reach it despite the very idea being anathema to the music.

There seemed no way for me to broach the subject with the male musicians. Try as I might to psych myself into walking up to one of the guys between sets and asking them about their compositions or how to get better at improvisation, I never could. Desperate to know their secrets, I listened at home for hours to their recordings, poring over liner notes like sacred texts. But at live gigs I was too self-conscious, obsessing over whether the musicians recognised me from my frequent attendance—and if they did, worrying that they thought I was a groupie looking for a date. I couldn't bear being thought of as a groupie even though I would have jumped at the chance of a date. Sex was the invisible and ubiquitous barrier to communication.

I submitted reviews of jazz gigs to the student newspaper, *Honi Soit*, and got a small buzz from seeing my name in print. If I couldn't be on stage, I thought, I could at least write about what I heard. For a time I co-presented a jazz show on campus radio with my new friend David, a Law student whose taste in jazz, as conservative as the rest of him, stopped at the soundtrack to *When Harry Met Sally*.

In her 2007 memoir *The Importance of Music to Girls*, Lavinia Greenlaw wrote, 'I knew there were those for whom music was soundtrack and those of us for whom it was, well, music, but didn't notice that most of those who took it seriously were boys.' My fascination with live jazz was as all-consuming as a love affair. Sublimation was the sincerest form of flattery—I needed regular live performances as other girls my age needed sex.

♫

I was not having sex with David. I was not interested in having sex with David. We enjoyed the sort of rapid-fire witty banter that young people too easily mistake for intimacy. The only men who really interested me were on stage, where they safely stayed and from where I could fantasise freely about our future together.

At nineteen, David already had the economic privilege and the testosterone to regard as inevitable a woman's hope to hitch her wagon to his breed of horse: private school education, budding lawyer, white. David and his classmates had gone from the elite Sydney Grammar School to the dorm rooms of St Paul's College in the collective movement of a school of fish. Having chosen to become lawyers and accountants like their fathers, they followed a career path as well signposted as a tourist trail. One hundred years after Banjo Paterson left Sydney Grammar to study Law, his fellow alumni were still becoming lawyers, if no longer writing poetry. Perhaps the loss of poetry reflected the process of sexual selection. David's professional future—which to him must have appeared linear as he walked those early qualifying steps along it—formed, when viewed from the distance of hindsight, a perfect circle.

'Career! That is all girls think of now, instead of being good wives and mothers and attending to their homes and doing what God intended,' rails Sybylla Melvyn's grandmother at the very mention of the C-word in *My Brilliant Career.* 'All they think of is gadding about and being fast, and ruining themselves body and soul.'

I would have loved to ruin myself body and soul, but in my first two years on campus there were no takers. At least none who interested me. For a long time it didn't occur to me that I kept people at arm's length: about the distance between a pianist and her instrument.

David laughed when I explained that I couldn't imagine ever marrying or having children. 'But you're studying for the marriage degree,' he teased about my poor-cousin qualification, the Bachelor of Arts. On some fundamental level, David was relieved to know his Law degree would grant him a vocational qualification, if not a sense of vocation. Perhaps what I really meant was that I would never marry him.

'You'd be a terrible mother anyway,' David said. This casual line stung me more in practice than it should have in theory, but I felt proud to confuse him.

Being single sounded just fine to me as long as I could find the roadmap that would show me what to do with my life. But I felt no closer to finding that map. Whether or not a young woman had marriage on her mind, at the close of the twentieth century, the Bachelor of Arts had become the contemporary equivalent of piano lessons.

25

Alice May Morrison Taylor's passport, which she presented on 25 August 1921 in order to embark the SS *Berrima*, lists the features of her 26-year-old face in a less-than-flattering light. *Forehead—square. Eyes: hazel. Nose: small. Mouth: medium. Chin: small. Colour of hair: dark. Complexion: ruddy. Face: round.* Next to the final item, *Any special peculiarities*, a short dash indicates there was nothing to add. What did my grandmother make of that dash? That there was nothing special about her, nothing to distinguish her round ruddy face from those of other women boarding a ship to the other side of the world? Experience had curdled the milky complexion of her schoolgirl portrait. Perhaps she felt the dash was appropriate. She most likely preferred to keep her peculiarity to herself: that dash was as conspicuous a silence as a period of rest marked on a music score.

Like Alice May Morrison Taylor herself, the SS *Berrima* was a product of the working classes of Glasgow. The workers of Caird & Co. at Greenock on the south side of the Clyde built the passenger liner in 1913 before the navy requisitioned it for less leisurely purposes.[54] In the roundabout way of these things, the ship travelled all the way to Sydney to be refitted and armed. And to push the irony even further, the *Berrima* was transformed in Sydney Harbour at the Cockatoo Island Dockyard—less than five hundred metres from the Hunters Hill peninsula where, sixty years later, I would grow up. Now an auxiliary cruiser, HMAS *Berrima* left Sydney on 19 August 1914 and headed to New Guinea, landing troops in September. Returning to Sydney, the *Berrima* changed roles again. She became a troop transport ship and sailed for the Middle East in December 1914. On 24 March 1920, the *Berrima* resumed commercial service.

Alice had made it to London—the Royal Docks at the Port of London, at any rate, a few twists of the Thames east from the city's centre. The girl from Glasgow had arrived in the music capital of her world, and no sooner had she set foot in it than she was boarding the gangway of the *Berrima* for a voyage of more than 13,000 miles.

Physically packing up her life wouldn't have taken much time. There wasn't much room at home for accumulating the sorts of things other young women drew to themselves like iron filings. Alice had her house clothes and her good clothes, and what she didn't have she knew how to make. In any event the *Berrima* had a strict baggage limit per passenger. The bulk of Alice's weight allowance was most likely taken up in copies of the church music repertoire, some of it as yellowed as the smoke-stained walls of the sitting room at 370 Dumbarton Road.

Perhaps there was music at the Docks that marked the beginning of Alice's journey; more likely she heard the percussion of mass travel—the wails of children, the sniffles of women, the thud of boots and the scrape of luggage—punctuated by the bellows of the mighty ship as the time neared for departure. She would never set foot in Covent Garden, or hear a concert at the Royal Academy of Music. There would be no scholarship to the Guildhall School or the Royal College of Music. There would be no position as a private music teacher for an aristocratic young lady while she undertook the grand tour. Alice would not become a governess for an upper middle-class family in London, or on one of the country estates where bored daughters idled their young lives away reading Jane Austen and waiting for a husband. I wonder if Alice thought about all the kindred musical spirits she might have met if she'd only had the opportunity to study and work in London, and if that knowledge was harder for her to bear than the thought of never seeing her brothers again.

There was no one on the Docks waving her goodbye. Who could have afforded the time and the travel for such an extravagant gesture? But perhaps she wished someone was waving her off who would miss her. She might have thought of the people she'd known in her life till now, and wondered why she was still by herself when other girls had found husbands. It couldn't be solely because she had chosen poorly in John Henry Edwards. Alice would have heard of similar stories often enough in the past three years to know bigamy was unfortunate but far from rare. Did she suspect that something was wrong with her? That her focus on music took up all the room where proper love for a husband should have been? That she had been so devastated and humiliated that she doubted she could believe the words of any man.

Thinking about Alice's decision to emigrate, I struggle to understand why she gave up her job at Gardner Street. Resigning from that coveted position would have been the biggest decision of Alice's life that she had made with complete information. Did she feel bereft or liberated? She knew no one at her destination with connections that might help her find the work for which she was best suited. And although she carried letters of recommendation, what significance would they be given by people unfamiliar with the institutions of her study and work? As the *Berrima* embarked on its seven-week voyage, I wonder if Alice considered that it had taken years for her to make her musical network, and that she was sailing away from those who could help her, recommend her, point her in the right direction. That while she'd married a sailor, it was she who had ended up at sea, floating to the bottom of the world.

I suspect my grandmother failed to value her skills as a musician. She most likely underestimated the value of her contribution to the musical life of her home town, even though she was a paid professional, being the choirmistress of two well-established churches and performing regularly as a soloist. She had suffered the humiliation of marrying a bigamist, but had continued to work during and after the scandal. I believe she lacked faith in her ability to go on making a living as a choirmistress; and that, coupled with the unspoken expectations of her family that she marry in order to secure her financial future, drove her from Glasgow to Australia.

♫

Alice's parents had not abandoned her. Charlotte and James Taylor were present for the momentous occasion of their daughter's departure for the new world—but not to wave her goodbye. Passenger records from the *Berrima* show that Charlotte and James boarded the ship in third class like their daughter. Unlike Alice, they held return tickets. On the passenger list, James Taylor's occupation is described as *boilermaker.* The self-designation seemed to indicate career progression of a sort, but to be a boilermaker was still back-breaking manual labour. Now in his fifties, he must have taken leave without pay from Denny's Shipyard in order to be able to spend several months away from home.

James and Charlotte had the excuse of visiting Nance and her family in Newcastle, but their decision to accompany Alice strikes me as a conscious if belated effort at protection and supervision. I'm not convinced they weren't suspicious that Alice was capable of disappearing—whether by melting into the crowds on her arrival at the Port of Sydney, or by throwing herself into the steely depths of the Atlantic.

26

AT NINETEEN, THE EXAMINATION FOR AN Associate of Music Diploma in Piano Performance loomed on the horizon as prominently as my virginity. A handsome 24-year-old tennis coach had recently offered to seduce me. His tone was that of a man bestowing a great favour, as if my innocence were as easily unzipped as the cover of my wooden Chris Evert racquet. Reader, I wish I could say that I let him, but I was too uptight to return his volley. Madame Bovary used her piano lessons as a ruse to meet her lover; but I used mine as a sublimation of lessons of an altogether different kind.

I channelled my sexual curiosity into piano study, interrogating the pieces my teacher had selected from the works considered suitably challenging by faceless music bureaucrats for the award of diploma. Mr McFarlane was best placed to identify those that suited my temperament and my technique. The A-Mus., as we abbreviated it, was of a different order of magnitude from the annual grade exams: to be eligible for the diploma, the candidate must have completed satisfactorily all grade exams in performance as well as a certified level of music theory. As I approached the summit of amateur musicianship, the sudden rise in the expected level of technical skill induced in me a kind of musical vertigo. A chiselled jaw or a pair of well-developed shoulders would only have caused my concentration to slip.

Frédéric Chopin's twelfth étude, known as the *Revolutionary Study*, opens with a declamatory five-note chord in the right hand and a run of semiquavers descending rapidly in the left. Like all études, this is a composition specifically designed to strengthen a pianist's technique. The demanding work isn't known as the *Revolutionary* for nothing. The Polish composer wrote it in despair on learning that the November 1830

Warsaw uprising, led by a group of young military officers against the occupying Russian Army, had failed. Chopin directs the pianist to play *allegro con fuoco*, or cheerfully with fire, which I interpreted as a highly ambivalent instruction along the lines of *grin and bear it*.

To open the *Revolutionary Study* was to encounter the sobering truth that despite more than ten years spent learning the language of music, some works required a native speaker's fluency that was still beyond my reach. There were too many notes to get under my fingers for me to imagine ever being able to play the piece with feeling and musicianship—let alone cheerfully, or with fire. Which was a bit of a problem considering I was set to perform it in competition at the Sydney Opera House in six months.

My emotional connection to the work was another challenge. I had got a long way on the combination of attention to detail, an obsession with technical improvement, and self-discipline. Despite my ability, the gap between technique and feeling had widened. I was struggling to fake a passionate attachment to the works I studied intensively. Performing Brahms, Bartók and Mozart for my annual exams was an exercise in displaying myself for third-party judgement on a functional, specialised level. Every year my examiners praised my ability to memorise long works and included marks for 'expression', but to my ears the production of a feeling—melancholy, passionate or militaristic—smacked always of artifice and cultivation. I knew how to produce the sound of such a feeling, irrespective of whether I felt it. This to me seemed a detached and cynical approach to music that I felt I should have loved intensely; it was little wonder that I considered myself a fraud at the piano. When playing the works of composers for whom I had the greatest affinity—Bach and Beethoven—it seemed on the contrary that my innate love of their structures and harmonies led me to express myself too much, so that I was always having to rein myself in.

Most interpreters of the *Revolutionary Study* focus on the technical demands made of the performer's left hand. These demands require the seamless legato playing of semiquaver passages that distinguishes a real pianist from a hack. My instinctual response to the challenge of there being too many notes and not enough time was still to rush through learning the piece as though I were frantically completing some last-minute Christmas shopping. It didn't matter whether I was eating, reading a novel or walking, I was always in a hurry. At the piano I couldn't understand anything in part unless I had first awkwardly embraced the whole. Beyond the piano stool, in the real world, I barely said boo without first carefully pondering the implications of a syllable. But at the piano I was cavalier and careless, riding roughshod over the delicate intricacies of melody, harmony and rhythm just to play the complete work poorly with both hands. Too often during practice my lazy fourth and fifth fingers would ride in the slipstream of their stronger siblings. Missed notes and wrong notes were the inevitable result.

'This is too difficult,' I finally complained to Mr McFarlane. It was one of the few times in our seven years together that I admitted what I felt about any of the pieces I studied with him. Intimacy was a kind of music I had yet to practise in public—or anywhere, really.

'No, it's not,' he said.

Clearly not every teacher remembers his first time with the *Revolutionary Study*. He sat behind me in a chrome chair upholstered in fuzzy grey carpet, a benevolent dictator fallen on hard times. And like Mr McFarlane himself, the new chair was wider than the rickety wooden one it had replaced. A few months back he'd stopped tucking in his white short-sleeved polyester shirts.

'You'll get there,' he'd say, 'just take it one day at a time.' But I was tiring of his clichéd encouragements. I might as well have complained to my parents: their uniform response to any expression of frustration or difficulty was the highly irritating 'You'll figure it out.' Even though they were mostly right, I had concluded long ago that asking anyone for help was futile.

I continued practising daily, coaxing the reluctant fingers of my left hand to gain fluidity and evenness in playing the *Revolutionary Study*'s long semiquaver passages. Oscar Wilde quipped that 'the typewriting machine, when played with expression, is not more annoying than the piano when played by a sister or near relation', and on reflection my repetitive keyboard exercises must have been one of the banes of my brother's adolescence. But no sooner had I surmounted the difficulty of the left-hand part than I realised the semiquavers' dense trees obscured the forest of an even greater challenge: the chord clusters in my right hand that announced the stirring main melody.

With typically dramatic flair, Chopin enunciated the melody in chords for the right hand of between three and five notes played at once, spread over the reach of an octave. That means my right thumb and little finger played the melody using two notes—actually the same note, eight notes apart—while my second, third or fourth fingers played the remaining notes of any complex chords. When the piece is performed properly, the effect is of a bell-like clarity from the obedient multi-voiced choir of the pianist's right hand. But achieving this effect isn't nearly as easy as it may sound. The melodic chord passages demand a dual function of the one hand. While my 'outside' fingers were occupied in hitting the melody notes with precision, my second, third and fourth fingers had either to step high above the keyboard, like a woman lifting the hem of her dress above the muck, or to stretch up and out over the notes as written, like a can-can dancer wearing the same dress. All of it at precisely the right tempo and at a volume that ranged from the softest piano to the loudest forte, or in the case of this work, *sforzando.*

There was no getting around the main problem: my right hand was too small for the job. My battered copy of J.S. Bach's *Two-Part Inventions* is dotted with my first teacher's amended notation for seven-year-old hands that could not yet stretch to a single octave. I often suspected that Johann Sebastian—whose pudgy face beneath a ridiculous wig stared out at me from the cover—was not impressed by his exercises being rewritten so that I could splay my undisciplined fingers across the modern keyboard. Now, although my fingers were extremely disciplined, the *Revolutionary Study* demanded that my right hand play four and five notes simultaneously across an octave. This required the dexterity of a crab's claws and a handspan of ten notes. In every sense of the word, it was a stretch.

About three months before the competition, a fleeting sensation of tightness in my right forearm began to come and go during my daily practice sessions. It usually appeared when I played a lot of fast notes, and sometimes during the running octaves in the *Revolutionary Study.* The feeling was most like muscle soreness, as if I had hit too many practice serves on the tennis court. Yet I thought little of it because the strain always receded. To interpret the Chopin with authority, or to hang an Associate of Music Diploma above my desk, meant many hours of training each week. The countless repetitions of the muscles of my hands, strenuously exerting themselves on the most unnatural of movements, was what being a serious piano student was all about.

The idea that some physical discomfort was the inevitable by-product of intensive practice felt natural to me. If the tightness disappeared as soon as I stopped playing, that meant I was working hard. Surely this was a good thing. In the house I grew up in, industriousness ran a close second to cleanliness. After so many years of discipline, it never occurred to me that my technique could be faulty. Assuming that such an error could be observed, I trusted that Mr McFarlane would have seen and corrected it. I deduced that my right forearm was fatigued from practising the consecutive octaves, and that I needed to accept and endure it. There was no point in mentioning it. What could my teacher do except express sympathy?

I also suspected that I was exaggerating the pain I had begun to feel. I had recently played the *Revolutionary Study* for my father's Rotary Club to give the work a public trial run one month out from the eisteddfod. Artistically, my performance had as much revolutionary spirit as a can of Coke, but it went off without a technical hitch. Maybe the stiffness in my arm was all in my head.

♫

The Chopin competition was scheduled to begin in a half-hour or so. I had hopped on the 506 bus to Circular Quay as if I travelled there every day, and arrived with plenty of time to turn myself into a nervous wreck. As I slowly made my way along the curving promenade towards the Opera House, my empty bladder insisted it was full. Perhaps I could register for the competition then hide in a toilet stall until show time. On my left, the green and gold ferries nodded encouragement from their watery berths. My black pants felt tight, and I fretted that the lines of my underpants would be visible beneath the stage lights.

Over the days leading up to the competition, the tension in my forearm had become increasingly severe. I'd hoped the sensation would go away of its own accord, but the tightness began seizing the muscles of my right forearm within minutes of practising the Chopin. Sometimes when I cleaned my teeth I would watch my right hand as it gripped the handle of the brush, making the same movements it made every morning; why was it that I could make these repetitive actions and incur no muscular penalty? At the piano, my right wrist began to feel sore and stiff too. From elbow to wrist my arm felt as if it was freezing over in a pianistic permafrost—as if it were the tip of a slow-moving, threatening force beneath the surface of my lightning fingers.

I had mentioned this problem to no one. Shame at my physical limitations as a pianist was a large part of my decision to remain silent, but I had no vocabulary to describe my vague and transitory symptoms. As far as I knew they had no name, and Mr McFarlane had noticed no change in my playing. Nor did it occur to me to withdraw from the competition—finishing things I had started, whether it was a novel or the food on my dinner plate, was a long-ingrained habit. I had agreed to compete with the best of my contemporaries, and I would show up as planned.

'Athletes of the small muscles.' That's what American pianist Leon Fleisher calls professional musicians, who ask extraordinary feats of their fingers and hands. Fleisher was a child prodigy who first performed on the concert stage at the age of eight. After almost twenty years of public performance, the fourth and fifth fingers of Fleisher's right hand started to curl in on each other as he practised passages of octaves in the Tchaikovsky First Concerto for a forthcoming tour. 'A hand can take only so much brutalisation before it starts to fight back,' he writes in his autobiography *My Nine Lives*. In 1963, with no one to advise him, Fleisher decided to address the problem by practising harder. But his right hand began to feel numb, and his fingers began to cramp. Within a year his career as a concert pianist was over.

♫

Inside the Opera Theatre, which seats 1500, perhaps forty friends and family of my competitors were scattered among the first dozen or so tiered rows behind the orchestra pit. Just twelve of us were playing the *Revolutionary Study* in competition, and eleven of them were wearing stony faces and Sydney Conservatorium of Music High School uniforms. I realised my solitude was no accident but a strategy to protect me from seeing disappointment in the eyes of those who thought me talented. Despite my regular accompanying, and without being conscious of it, over the course of my high school years I'd grown to associate playing the piano with being alone. It was a safe, controlled, isolated environment. Like a bell-jar.

The first competitor walked on to the stage. He was so petite that a strong gust of wind could have knocked him sideways, but he approached the piano with a confident stride. I wondered if the Conservatorium high school taught him to do that or if it came naturally. When he sat down he spent what felt like a great deal of time adjusting the stool, just as every concert pianist I'd seen had done. Before he'd touched a single note I was completely intimidated.

He executed the *Revolutionary Study* not only with fire, but also the precision of a machine gun. I hadn't even played yet and it was all over. As I listened to his faultless interpretation, I diagnosed myself as a fraud. My competitors had chosen to study classical music with such dedication that they had competed successfully for a place at the Conservatorium high school, the main talent pipeline for the Conservatorium of Music. At some critical moment each of these teenagers had decided to pursue classical piano performance exclusively, and had taken what felt to me an almost religious vow by joining the Order of the Conservatorium. The idea of forsaking all other creative possibilities, which was how I regarded their commitment to the classical repertoire, felt like a death. I must have shared a high level of technical skill with my competitors to have propelled me into the ranks of advanced amateurs. But as I heard a succession of good to excellent Chopin interpreters, I understood that their superior ability wasn't simply a matter of greater dexterity than mine, or more hours devoted to practice: they were passionately attached to their repertoire, whereas Chopin was what I practised in between teaching myself songs by the composers I preferred listening to, such as George Gershwin and Duke Ellington. To perform the *Revolutionary Study* in public was for me an intellectual challenge rather than an expression of monogamous love. Simply willing myself across the line would never work.

Finally my turn came. I stepped onto the stage of the Opera Theatre and sat at the prow of the gleaming Steinway. I felt the sharp heat of the stage lights on the back of my neck and a cold weight in my abdomen. In the piano's polished black surface I saw my own reflection. An uncanny sense of familiarity and novelty dazzled me. That long moment before I started playing was the culmination of all the hours and months and years of practice that had brought me here. I had done the work—sometimes joyful, often grinding—that enabled me to compete today. Perhaps I wasn't at my competitors' level, but I knew the *Revolutionary Study* inside out, and in a sense that was enough. My goal was to play the piece through with no mistakes, as if the pain that I had come to associate with this composition had been a hallucination. In *The Piano Teacher*, Erika Kohut tries to 'talk a blue streak about interpretation' to her students, but 'the only thing the students wish to do is play the piece correctly to the end'. Like me, they 'are afraid that when they play at the examination, their sweaty, fear-filled fingers . . . will slip to the wrong keys'. In my focus on technique rather than emotional expression, I had become the worst kind of piano student.

Adjusting the puckered leather stool to a comfortable distance, I began.

Almost as soon as I sounded the declarative octaves of the powerful melody, the familiar painful stiffness arrived. It came earlier than I had ever experienced it during private practice. My forearm felt as if I was trying to lift a dead weight, while my fingers tried to ignore what held them back. I played on, willing my arm to continue despite the slow icing-over that for the first time began to freeze the fourth and fifth fingers of my right hand.

To any rational pianist this creeping immobilisation would have signalled imminent disaster. In my mind's eye I was only on the third page of seven, but it was obvious to everyone present that something was terribly wrong. The severity of the stiffness was making me botch notes I'd never missed before. Chopin's étude, intended to help develop a pianist's technique, had hastened the deterioration of mine.

In the sequence leading up to the second articulation of the melody, during which the hands race down the keyboard in parallel motion, my right hand stopped functioning. The fingers, now fused and curled in on themselves from the stiffness in my wrist, could no longer move independently of each other. My forearm was locked in paralysis too. But my useless claw didn't stop moving: it skidded, taking my forearm with it, thundering across the treble keyboard in a hail of discordant notes.

Somehow I limped through the final bars. One still had to finish even if one were, in another sense, already finished.

The silence in the Opera Theatre was cold and complete. I did not expect comfort from these strangers, but I wished the spotlights would go dark. The humiliation radiated from me so powerfully that it felt as if my freckles were burning. Glancing briefly through the dusty haze of the stage lights, I saw the shadowy outlines of the Conservatorium students hunched together, nudging each other with their elbows like the undulations of a piano accordion. At least they had the decency not to laugh out loud. I had to get out of there before their silence burst.

I closed my eyes as I dipped my head in mortified farewell. A few sympathetic members of the audience clapped to congratulate me for finishing. The rest were too appalled to respond.

It wasn't until twenty years later, reading the story of Leon Fleisher for the first time in the neurologist Oliver Sacks's *Musicophilia*, that I recognised my experience and learned its name: focal dystonia, commonly known as musician's or writer's cramp. Some neurologists believe that the localised paralysis is the result of over-practice, during which the brain distorts the mental representation of the fingers such that they overlap and can't be controlled independently. Focal dystonia disproportionately affects musicians, most frequently pianists, violinists and guitarists, although it also strikes horn players' embouchure. Instead of maintaining a reciprocal balance between agonist and antagonist muscles, relaxing and contracting in tandem, the muscles contract together. It's as though the brain reaches a point, after countless repetitions of the fingers making the same movement, beyond which it can no longer differentiate the working of one finger from that of another on the same hand. If you think of a trill, in which two fingers manipulate two neighbouring keys at high speed; or the precise levering of the right hand required to play consecutive octaves, you can marvel at the brain's capacity to engineer these dexterous feats while empathising with its occasional failure to distinguish one performing finger from another. Research has shown that when parts of the somatosensory cortex, the section of the brain responsible for the sense of touch, repeatedly receive signals extremely close together, they can blur, perceiving the signals as simultaneous.[55] Fleisher believes that inappropriate practice techniques, rather than too much practice, are to blame for the task-specific paralysis. In any event, the debilitating cramp is a neurological more than a muscular affliction. The real problem wasn't in the muscles of my right arm: it was in my brain.

In 1831, the year that Chopin composed the *Revolutionary Study*, Robert Schumann began to experience cramping in the middle finger of his right hand. At twenty-one he was considered one of Europe's most promising virtuoso pianists.

Terrified of what this inexplicable development meant for his performing career, Schumann turned in desperation to a finger-stretching device. Unfortunately his loss of motor control in the 'bird' finger became worse, and within two years he abandoned performing. Today Schumann is best known as one of the finest composers of the Romantic period. His *Toccata* is the only work of the virtuoso piano repertoire that has no use for the third finger of the right hand. Clara Schumann became the first, and foremost, interpreter of her husband's works for piano.

Schumann's is the first known case of focal dystonia—in his case, the loss of task-specific motor control in the middle finger of his right hand while playing. According to contemporary neurologists, dystonia affects approximately one per cent of professional musicians, and Schumann displayed several of the disorder's primary risk factors: namely that he was a perfectionist, a man, and someone who was prone to anxiety and who practised for extended periods music that placed an extreme burden on the motor skills of the brain.[56] The only risk factor I was missing was a penis.

Leon Fleisher tried everything from homeopathy to hypnosis to fix his disobedient right hand. Some doctors thought he had a pinched nerve and wanted to operate on his spine. Many suspected that the problem was psychological. Despite his dystonia, Fleisher's devotion to the piano led him to become the world's leading performer of the repertoire that exists for the left hand.

Paul Wittgenstein, brother of philosopher Ludwig, was a promising pianist from a wealthy family who lost his right arm during World War I. After the war he commissioned concertos for the left hand from composers including Ravel, Hindemith and Prokofiev. The Ravel became Fleisher's signature solo work in one-handed recitals. But he never lost hope of performing again with two hands.

In the late 1980s researchers discovered that small injections of botox can block the nerve signals causing muscles to contract, and in the case of some musicians can help their muscles relax to a level that allows some to resume playing. The effect is temporary, just as it is for those who receive botox injections to relax the facial muscles that cause crow's-feet. Fleisher was one of the lucky ones: following injections into his right forearm, he played with both hands in a concert with the Cleveland Orchestra in 1996. It was thirty years since his last two-handed performance. Botox didn't prevent Leon Fleisher from ageing, but it did help him turn back the clock.

♫

When I left the Sydney Opera House after the Chopin competition, an undeniable relief punctured my humiliation. The experience had forced me to admit to myself that I didn't love the works I was studying so intensively for my A. Mus. A. diploma; that I strongly preferred playing jazz standards and trying, however poorly, to improvise; and that there was therefore little point in continuing my pursuit of a level of technical perfection that I couldn't achieve, and which, more importantly, I knew I did not want.

I would not be a classical pianist when I grew up. Not only did I lack the passionate dedication for such a life, but there was a physical limit to my ability to achieve it. And in terms of classical piano prodigies, I was already well over the hill.

My right hand had staged an uprising against the excessive demands I had made of it. Unlike Leon Fleisher, I wasn't prepared to fight this. It took me twenty years to learn that focal dystonia is a kind of rebellion of the body, but the discovery made perfect sense. As a teenager I had agreed, deep down, with what my body was telling me, but had tried very hard to ignore it. It was the only powerful force in my life that I had refused immediately to obey.

Perhaps at this point other students would have tossed in the piano altogether, but the goal of obtaining my performance diploma remained. It was only a month or three away, I reasoned with myself, constitutionally unable to abandon a goal once set. And so I turned up to my weekly lessons with Mr McFarlane, kept practising at home—where the dystonia disappeared now that we had substituted a Brahms prelude for the Chopin—and dutifully passed my A. Mus. A. exam on 25 November 1989.

'Memory work is commended. There was a sense of performance but do be careful not to allow the audience to be aware by your "grimaces" of everything you are not pleased with in your playing,' noted one of the two examiners in her handwritten report.

♫

Recently, my friend Kelsey and I discussed our musical adventures in high school. She is the only person from school I keep in touch with, but not only because we were expat Australians in the USA. As teenagers we'd spent a lot of time together rehearsing pieces for her to sing at school concerts with my accompaniment, from Schubert arias through to Lennon and McCartney.

'I remember listening to you perform when you first arrived at Wenona,' she recalled. 'The headmistress asked you to play for the school, and it sounded amazing. I thought, *Who on earth is that?*'

It's funny what you choose to remember. I had no recollection of the performance.

'But I have to tell you,' Kelsey said, 'you never looked happy when you played.'

In *This Real Night*, Rose Aubrey despairs of a new piano teacher who insists she go back to the fundamentals of study.

In her despair, Rose considers the tantalising prospect of abandoning the instrument altogether.

> For as I sobbed I was only partly anguished. I also saw a vision of myself walking by the river near the Dog and Duck, as happy as the blessed dead, my mind flowing bright and unconfined and leisured as the Thames I looked on, because I had cast away the burden, so infinitely greater than myself who had to bear it, of my vocation. I would earn a living somehow.

Though I was never going to be a concert pianist, and though I'd never felt convinced beyond doubt that the piano was my vocation, I felt the liberation of having cast away the burden West describes. But it wasn't until I discontinued lessons with Mr McFarlane and stopped practising my scales and arpeggios, my Mozart K280, my Bach 'Prelude and Fugue in F minor', my Brahms 'Rhapsody' and my Prokofiev 'Gavotte', that I felt how heavy and unreasonable my self-imposed burden of solo piano performance had been. After almost thirteen years, my highwire act riding the tension monocycle was over. Now, like Rose Aubrey, I'd have to think about ways to earn a living. I was studying for an Arts degree. I was still living at home. And, on the cusp of twenty, I was still a virgin.

27

As the Berrima *ploughed its way through the South Atlantic Ocean, Alice came to enjoy strolling the deck by herself after dinner with nothing but the depthless water below her and the stars above. On deck she avoided the couples who colonised the bow with their linked arms and their two abreast, preferring to stop halfway along the ship where its sooty exhalations were at their thinnest no matter which way the wind blew. She liked to inhale deeply and watch the wind whip the waves into stiff peaks; she found staring into the brilliantly lit nothingness unexpectedly soothing, the whoosh and slap of the water against the ship a reassuring sound of literal progress, even if she felt that she personally was making little.*

According to that morning's announcement during breakfast, they were but a few days from the port of Cape Town. How the crew knew that was beyond her, though every passenger was keenly aware that rounding the Cape of Good Hope represented the halfway mark of their voyage.

For years Alice had felt she was always being observed and judged, whether it was by her family, her music teachers, her neighbours or her choir. Even here, looking out on the middle of nowhere, she was surprised to feel surrounded, though it was by water. The crucial difference, Alice realised, was that while standing alone gazing outwards, observation flowed in one direction only. The stars weren't watching her, nor was the sea waiting for her to fall in. The feeling of complete anonymity against the immense silence of sea and sky was intoxicating.

How long the tall fellow had been looking at her before she noticed him, Alice had no idea. He was very thin, with narrow shoulders and what was possibly a slight stoop, though it could easily have been an illusion produced by his leaning into the strong wind that gusted along the deck. The bones protruded from his face as if he were some hastily assembled piece of machinery. He wore a tweed flat cap in a herringbone pattern and regarded her patiently through wire-rimmed spectacles in the manner of someone who, although Alice hadn't met him, seemed to know exactly who she was.

Instantly he reminded her of the man she'd not seen in years but who haunted her dreams—and of whom, despite her best efforts, she hadn't quite been able to train herself to stop thinking.

Alice nodded at the thin man before turning back towards the ocean, reminding herself it was pointless and fanciful to entertain notions about a complete stranger. Look how far that had got her last time. With each wave the ship crested and sank, a pattern as common to music as to heartbreak. When Alice turned back the man was no longer there.

♫

Once or twice since their encounter on the deck, Alice had nodded in acknowledgement at the hollow-cheeked man with the spectacles. She had noticed him during the dinner service, sitting with a few other seemingly unattached men at a table not far from her own, where she endured the talk with fellow travellers that grew smaller each meal. And she had seen him at the rear of the chapel when she was leaving after the service. His shyness radiated towards her, and Alice sensed that it would take only the smallest encouragement from her to see him walk awkwardly in her direction, all limbs and bony shoulders, to introduce himself. It amused her to think that just minutes earlier she had been singing in her clear soprano voice, and yet now she chose to remain silent. Choosing not to speak was a power of sorts, she supposed. She feared being bored immediately by the man with hope in his eyes. But perhaps her deeper fear was the return of hope in her own.

A few nights later Alice arrived at dinner to find him sitting next to her father, comparing the food heaped on their plates. She was impressed: her father's powers of observation were greater than she had given him credit for. In his nervousness he stood up too fast, bumping the table so that the nearest drinks wobbled.

James Taylor introduced his daughter to Mr George Lloyd. 'Mr Lloyd here's returning from Cardiff, where he's been visiting his mother.'

Alice was surprised to learn that he was a farmer's labourer. He looked more the indoors type.

'I was working out at Suntop farm, west of Yeoval district, saving up for my own lease,' he said. 'But there's no place like home, is there?'

Alice wasn't so sure. She was looking forward to the opportunity to miss it.

She felt sorry for the softly spoken man and wanted to put him at ease. He hunched over slightly when he talked, which made her suspect he was self-conscious about his height. His slender hands and elongated fingers looked better suited to a librarian or a pianist, though the tops of his hands appeared more wrinkled than she would have expected of someone his age. What was his age, anyway? About forty, maybe, though Nance had written that many locals looked older than their years due to the intensity of the Australian sun. Perhaps thirty-six. Who was she to be picky, at hers?

And did George enjoy the line of work he had chosen? After watching her father and brothers spend their working lives as human fodder for shipbuilders, Alice couldn't help but respect a man for wanting to be his own boss. And if he was still rake-thin after eating his mother's meals for six months, George would never develop a belly like her father's, sagging over his pants like excess baggage. George's suit jacket hung off him as if it was pegged on a line.

Alice could tell George was dying to ask her what her plans were once they made it to Sydney. Any fantasy of staying aloof and mysterious evaporated with the ensuing line of conversation, in which her mother shared that her son-in-law would pick them up in Sydney and escort them on the train to Newcastle.

'Why, that's only three hours from Yeoval!' George exclaimed, failing to temper his excitement.

Despite herself, Alice found his ineptitude charming. She liked how his eyes creased at their edges when he smiled. It gave her the sense that they'd had a lot of practice. Beyond the superficial resemblance, she thought, he really was nothing like John Henry Edwards. George could no more tell a lie or disguise his true intentions than he could hold back the tide. There was no deviation from the norm, no hidden nuances or secret agendas. George Lloyd was as straight as a cricket bat.

♫

Alice emerged from her 10,000-mile odyssey with a suitcase, a shy suitor and a glimmer of hope. Though she was ten years younger than George, I suspect what she had learned about men and love had given her an edge on her future husband. Growing up, I never heard one rose-coloured narrative around the family Christmas dinner table of their shipboard meeting, or apocryphal stories of their courtship.

Despite the romance that retrospect can too readily supply, my sense is that it wasn't a primary motivator for either party.

For George, a lifetime bachelor with few prospects of finding a wife, the ship must have offered several opportunities to meet young women. But most of them would already have been attached to husbands, whether present or waiting for them in Sydney. So to meet Alice, unmarried and relatively old, must have struck George as an unexpected stroke of fortune. With poor eyesight and few assets of his own, he wasn't exactly a prime candidate for a young woman's affections; after all, for most women marriage was the biggest financial decision of their lives. But Alice was different: she wasn't impressed by shows of wealth or displays of charm. She had once made the mistake of confusing them for genuine affection. What she was looking for was trustworthiness, reliability, steadfastness, sincerity—qualities that to an inexperienced girl in the flush of romance might appear dull, but shone steadily as moonlight to a woman whose life had changed forever because of their absence. After a long time spent travelling over a bottomless ocean, Alice's feet once again touched solid ground.

George returned to his farm, and Alice secured a job cleaning a guesthouse not far from Nance's home in the suburb of Merewether. The two corresponded for eight months before George formally proposed on his second visit to Newcastle. In 1922 Alice May Morrison Taylor disappeared for the second time. She became Mrs Alice Lloyd of Yeoval, New South Wales.

28

After two years of platonic friendship, David's persistent charm and sense of humour had coaxed me from my metaphorical piano stool. Though I now called him my boyfriend, and was working three jobs so we could travel together after I finished my degree at the end of the year, our physical relationship was such a disappointment that I often regretted straying from the piano.

From a wobbly start to undergraduate study, I had worked out how to write for my professors. I completed a four-year honours degree in English Literature with a long essay on jazz poetry by Langston Hughes, Mina Loy and Philip Larkin. I was inspired by writers whose work in turn was inspired by musicians who sounded like nobody else. My fevered passion for jazz, which had only intensified after my abandonment of serious piano study, was channelled into my research. Theoretically speaking, the essay wasn't sophisticated, but as an act of sublimation, it was total.

Having accidentally timed my graduation to coincide with the recession that the then Australian prime minister told us 'we had to have', I emerged with high marks and low prospects. My first-class Bachelor of Arts degree carried about the same vocational value as a coupon from a packet of cornflakes. But ever the ostrich, I decided not to worry about a job until I returned from my travels in the new year. What a luxury to be able to make that decision, I think now.

While we were overseas, David and I heard a lot of jazz: the Chick Corea Elektric Band in San Francisco, our first stop; unnamed musicians at Chumley's speakeasy in New York, where my jaw dropped on first sight of the Manhattan I'd dreamed of for years, and pretty much stayed open every day we were there; and a trad jazz band at Le Caveau in Paris.

I was grateful for the hospitality of David's extended family—we had places to stay in expensive cities, and meals we didn't have to pay for—but I couldn't shake the growing realisation that he and I weren't a good match. My savings quickly dwindled, and I dreaded having to ask my parents for a temporary loan to get me home. David didn't understand my concern; he was neither cautious with his travel money, nor concerned about how to access more. Unlike me, he hadn't worked like mad around his classes to save up. Still studying Law and living at St Paul's College, he worked no job. He'd simply asked his grandmother for the money, and she had given it to him.

By the time I was ready to come home, which was still ten long and expensive days before the date printed on my ticket, I'd decided our relationship was over. But in Rome, on the final leg of our journey, David shocked me by announcing he thought it was a good idea that we move in together. That night, whether prompted by a dodgy dinner or by his declaration, I went to the bathroom and was violently ill. Once again I was lying to myself and, by extension, to David. But I couldn't afford to change my flight. I would end it when we got home.

During the trip, I sometimes phoned my parents to assure them that I was still alive. During one of those brief conversations, my mother informed me that I'd been offered a scholarship to undertake a graduate research degree at the University of Sydney: a meagre stipend that would pay for me to complete a Masters in English Literature, or an unimaginable PhD down the track. But there was a deadline for responding to the offer, which would close before I returned to Sydney. Without thinking too much—other than how handy it was to have that up my sleeve while I tried to get a real job—I asked my mother to accept the offer on my behalf.

When I got back, I discovered that I wasn't the only one who had been omitting key information in the mistaken belief it was in the best interests of another person. My parents had chosen not to let me know that my brother, now eighteen, had been unexpectedly hospitalised for ten days while I was traipsing around Europe. 'We didn't want to spoil your trip,' they explained. My love for my brother aside, I could have used an excuse to cut my trip short.

29

ALICE WOULD NEVER FORGET THE SIGHT of that poor piano arriving at Devon Farm, strapped to the top of a horse-drawn cart like a prisoner. The black upright was held in place with a complicated arrangement of canvas straps and ropes with knots and blankets to prevent the ropes from chafing it. From her kitchen window she watched the instrument sway and dip as the horses brought it nearer. What had it done to end up here in the middle of nowhere, she wondered as it lurched towards her. Of all the things they needed in this faithless dustbowl, and George organises for her to have a piano.

The heaving cart came to a stop not far from the back door, and the piano tilted forward at a slight angle, as if straining to be free of its shackles. She cringed at the thought of how out of tune it would be, while George hurried over to the driver, letting the flyscreen slam behind him. 'Sorry!' he yelled over his shoulder at his wife. She shut her eyes tightly to mitigate the sound. She had tried in vain to discourage George's habit, especially in the six months since Charlotte was born.

On cue, the baby started wailing in her cot. Alice knew she had only a minute or two before the cries reached their crescendo, when she'd have no choice but to pick up Charlotte and try to placate her. Two minutes was time enough to start a batch of scones, Alice decided. The men would be expecting tea when they were done moving the piano.

The sifted flour made dunes in the mixing bowl as Alice observed her husband through the window, trying to decipher his easy way with strangers. The firm handshake, the instant smile, the nodding, the skywards glance followed by what she assumed, based on experience, to be banal observations of the day's weather—put together like a sequence of dance steps, George's actions provided comfort of a kind she neither sought nor offered. Charlotte's wails were insistent. Alice wiped her hands on her apron. The men would have to wait.

By the time she returned with the baby on her hip, George and the driver had untied the piano and coaxed it down a ramp covered in a faded rug. It would still be half an hour before they had cajoled it inside the house. Alice placed Charlotte in her bassinet on the kitchen floor while she finished making the scones and popped them in the oven. Unless she was wet or hungry, the baby girl cried little and seemed content to keep herself company. Alice found the latter both a point of pride and an enormous relief.

Charlotte's fascination with every detail of her new life bewildered Alice. The baby stared contentedly at the ceiling cornices, the windowsills, the tap in the kitchen sink, and at the afternoon shadow cast by the wardrobe in Alice's bedroom. When Alice looked around her, all she saw was dust. The dust was everywhere—in the sheets, the cutlery drawer, in her eyes, on her tongue and inside her nose. She fought it despite the feeling that the dancing motes mocked her efforts.

George and the driver groaned with the effort of lifting and sliding the piano using a combination of rugs and blankets. George caught Alice's eye as he squatted for a moment in the kitchen doorway to catch his breath. He looked from her to the baby, smiling. 'I thought the sitting room . . . ?' he said. She supposed he was looking for a gesture of gratitude or pleasure. She nodded. What could she say? All her life she had dreamed of having her own piano. Now here it stood, a jet-black colt restrained by two handlers, and it was as out of place and trapped as she was.

While the men positioned the instrument in the darkest corner of the front room, Alice set out the tea and scones. The driver had the sense to consume two scones and a cup of scalding black tea quickly before leaving the friendly farmer to his stern-faced wife.

'I thought you'd be happy,' George said into his teacup, once the rattle of the departing cart had faded.

'I am,' she said, thinking how words covered over the truth of things like the paperbark over the cool trunks of the gum trees. 'Just . . . surprised, that's all.' She put her hand on George's shoulder and softened her expression.

He looked up at her quickly, as she had expected him to do, seeking permission for the next step, which was to reach for her hand and squeeze it. A husband, afraid of his own wife. She didn't know whether to cry, or laugh in his face.

Alice felt the gulf between them, as vast as the ocean she had crossed, but had no clue how to bridge it even if she'd wanted to. George would expect her to welcome him into her bed tonight. He rarely dared approach her since the baby arrived, and because of the piano she felt she could not say no. She found the physical act itself unremarkable, if messy; what she feared lay beyond the realm of the senses, too easily deceived, in the invisible country of intimacy. It was a land to which she seemed to be refused entry. This time she hoped to have a boy.

Alice sat down to familiarise herself with the piano, George's eyes hot on the back of her neck. It didn't feel like she had imagined it would, having a piano of her own at last. The piano room of her dreams was devoted to music, with a gramophone in the corner opposite the instrument, etchings of the great composers hung on one wall, and shelves stacked neatly with choral arrangements. On Devon Farm, the piano competed for space with a large wireless, a settee and a big basket of wool punctured with crochet and knitting needles. She wanted to disappear at the piano, to slide down the rabbit hole on her fingertips to a musical world of her own making, like she used to do when she was a girl and her brothers were running amok. Instead she was the focus of her husband's attention.

Alice didn't care for the reflection the instrument cast back at her. In her home-made apron and with her permanent cigarette, she reminded herself of no one more than her mother. Despite the heat of the afternoon, the ivory keys were cool to her fingertips. She did her best not to flinch at how flat the notes were. At first her fingers felt like dancers who couldn't remember their routine. But slowly they found their way through some of the old Scottish songs, and the notated music formed a picture in her mind's eye as clear as John Henry Edwards' face. At the end of each piece, Alice recalled, was the same instruction. Da capo, *it said. Return to the beginning.*

'Maybe you'll teach Charlotte to play, when she's old enough,' came George's voice behind her. Until this moment Alice hadn't thought about her daughter learning the instrument, and was shocked to feel her stomach lurch at the idea.

When she'd told George that she was expecting a baby, he had choked back tears and suggested that they should name a girl after Alice's mother. She had smiled and nodded her agreement, thinking how impossible it was to make a fresh start of anything in life. At the end of everything was da capo.

30

'GET OVER THERE, THEY WON'T BITE ya,' said Freddy Wilson, shooing me to the far left corner of the converted garage at the back of his garden in Boronia Park, a leafy suburb a few minutes from the one where I had grown up.

I picked my way between wonky music stands and chipped coffee mugs to the electronic keyboard and sat on a black stool whose torn vinyl seat had padded years of bottoms. To my immediate left was standing-room only for the double-bass player and his instrument, as long as he didn't swing too literally. And on his left, in the far right corner of the garage, sat the drummer at his kit. I had finally become the piano player in a jazz band, and I felt as hip as a prosthesis.

I'd had to wait some months for a place in one of Freddy's weekly amateur jazz workshops, which gave singers and instrumental soloists the rare opportunity to perform live with a rhythm section. The diminutive drummer had been a band leader and arranger in the big band heyday of the 1950s and 60s. Since then, Freddy and his wife Bev had been running workshops for singers and instrumentalists from their home. Slim and weathered, Bev towered over her husband. When I'd showed up early for the first night of the ten-week term, she had greeted me like a long-lost friend and ushered me inside, where a handful of other new students perched on an ad hoc arrangement of chairs, sipping instant coffee.

Ten minutes later the flyscreen door that gave on to the rear porch slid open to admit Freddy Wilson himself. Immune to the conventional repertoire of human facial expression, Freddy offered newcomers only a grunt, an upward nod and a raised eyebrow. We trudged across the illuminated lawn behind him like a trail of ants towards the single-car garage that had been reborn as a rehearsal space. Grey carpet lined the walls in an effort to muffle the sound. Besides the rhythm section of keyboard, acoustic bass and drums were a saxophone player, a trumpeter, an acoustic guitarist and three singers. Fresh air wafted into the garage only when the door opened to admit a latecomer. The singers lined up on stools near the door waiting their turn under the extreme lighting, which would have been sufficient to power a small aircraft.

After a quick point-and-name introduction of each participant, Freddy got down to business.

'Yeah, everyone. Listen up. Here's how it works,' he began with a tap of his cigarette. 'The singers get two songs each, one at a time. Band members, you get a solo of two choruses, one for each song. Work out among yourselves who's going first.' A neglected ashtray sat on the edge of a bookshelf in easy tipping reach. Freddy preferred to let his embers fall to the concrete floor where they joined a general smudge at his feet. He ran on cigarette smoke and coffee for the duration of the two-hour workshop, and the garage door remained closed. 'Okay, singers, who's gonna be first? How 'bout you, Lisa? Whatcha doing tonight?'

'"Cry Me a River",' Lisa said, pulling at her underpants through her faded jeans as she stood up.

'All right.' Freddy rummaged in a deep cardboard box whose corners were reinforced with duct tape, his cigarette dangling from one corner of his downturned mouth, searching for the music charts to hand out to everyone. Though the singers were mostly women, I was the only female member of the band.

The one-page chart for 'Cry Me a River' showed only the melody on a series of treble staves and the chords underpinning it, each marked by its quality—C-6 or E♭Maj7, for example—in a kind of Esperanto for accompanying and improvising. I propped the sheet on the keyboard's rickety music stand, thrilled that my years of mucking around at home by myself with Fake Books had not been in vain.

For a jazz standard, 'Cry Me a River' begins on a relatively high first note, the sixth of the tonic or home key, and is held for the first two beats of the four-bar measure while the singer vocalises the first word: 'Now'. Which wouldn't be too high a bar to fly over were it not for the fact that the diphthong 'ow' is difficult to sing even without a broad Australian accent, or that the song is a ballad, and slower songs are notoriously harder to get right than faster ones. One of the most-recorded abandoned-lover laments, 'Cry Me a River' is paradoxically both more difficult to sing than it appears, and a standard of choice for beginner jazz singers. In other spheres of the performing arts, technical complexity would be enough to discourage beginners—because of, say, the threat of physical pain in the case of a ballet dancer attempting a pirouette en pointe. But of course, anyone who has a voice can attempt to sing anything.

'Know the lyrics yet?' Freddy asked Lisa.

She rolled her eyes. 'Freddy!'

'Christ, Lisa. Yer gotta know the words. No excuses.'

Freddy counted us in. 'Ah-one, ah-two, ah-one-two-three-ugh!' We played a four-bar introduction before Lisa wobbled on the first word like a tightrope walker about to lose her footing.

After Lisa careened through one chorus, meaning the full thirty-two bars of the song, the instrumentalists took solos from the head in the conventional manner of the jazz ensemble. To take a solo means to create spontaneously a musical idea and play for the duration of one or more choruses—to improvise based on some combination of the harmonic structure, the melody and the rhythm of the song. I had never done this with other musicians, but it was exactly why I'd been drawn to these workshops. Despite my heart being stuck in my throat, I couldn't wait to solo. Fortunately, for the first chorus the saxophone player took the solo, so I had extra time to think about the structure of the song.

'Cry Me a River' has a conventional AABA jazz standard pattern, with its thirty-two bars split into two lots of eight (A), a bridge (B) of eight bars, and a final eight-bar section to finish (A). If you know a song with such a structure well enough, you intuitively hear that pattern without being conscious of it. Ideally, that means when you perform it you don't have to think about counting numbers of bars, or whether you're on the first or second eight of the A section, or where you are in the bridge. Needless to say, in Freddy's workshops I did a lot of counting, very loudly, inside my head. There was also a lot of heel-tapping with my right foot, and whacking of my left calf muscle against the stool I sat on.

While it sounds as though I spent my whole performance stuck in my head counting bars, I didn't—there just wasn't time. I'd hardly got started with my solo when it was all over. It was someone else's turn in the 32-bar spotlight. The beautiful thing is that even when one of us forgot where we were in the song, or got lost in the middle, somehow the rest of the band carried us in its current. We could re-enter the stream when we regained our footing, without too much disruption to the overall momentum.

My relief at not having to be perfect was exhilarating. Here was a way to play the piano with others, and not have to memorise twenty minutes of intricately annotated music, and not have to reproduce it perfectly and the same way each time I played it.

After the instrumentalists had each taken their solo, Lisa sang another chorus before we came to the end.

'Well that was a fuckin' train wreck, wasn't it?!' said Freddy, looking back and grinning at the other singers-in-waiting who had just clapped their appreciation for Lisa's effort. He pointed his cigarette at them and raised his bushy eyebrows for emphasis. 'Remember, a short note's a good note.'

Lisa nodded, unfazed.

'Take it again, from the top.'

Freddy's method was nothing if not consistent. First he'd fix you with his death stare, then offer a few brief but tasty phrases through a mouth that barely moved:

'Yeah, good, but yer too slow. It's not a fuckin' funeral.'

'What happened to you?'

'Don't be afraid not to play.'

'Yer gotta be yerself.'

Freddy wasn't interested in contemporary jazz, which he defined as anything composed after 1959. He'd already seen and heard everyone he believed worth hearing. 'They're all up their own arses as far as I'm concerned,' he said, referring to Miles Davis and *Kind of Blue*.

I didn't want to be myself. I wanted to be able to play exactly like Bill Evans, who had begun by studying classical piano, and ended up as one of the twentieth century's most influential improvisers and composers. His nuanced chord voicings on *Kind of Blue* were a large part of Miles Davis's phenomenal success with that album, despite Freddy's tin ear for the landmark recording. In a 1966 documentary made by his brother Harry, Bill confessed that when he first began improvising, he considered that he'd done well if he had played one note differently from how a piece had been notated. One note! And here I was, having deviated from the notated music almost as soon as I'd started reading it, never daring to pursue it seriously through all these years of playing.

I wonder if I'd had a different teacher, studied a different repertoire, not focused on the annual grade exams, if that might have led me to study improvisation and become a professional musician. If only I had seen that documentary when I was thirteen, I say to myself sometimes, fantasising about what it might have been like to live the life of a jazz musician in New York—at the same time knowing that, even if I'd had the chops, it was a life I would never have had the courage to lead. It was a life Bill Evans himself, despite his distinctive harmonic voicings and startlingly original compositions, found impossible to lead without heroin and later cocaine, both of which contributed to his death at fifty-one in 1980.

♫

Outside the confines of Freddy's garage, I had formed the distinct impression that everyone else I knew had a firm idea of what they wanted to do with their lives. Friends were becoming lawyers, radio producers, journalists, book editors. Acquaintances were morphing into architects or political consultants, or going into the family business. They were working and earning a living. I, on the other hand, was pursuing a graduate degree in English Literature.

I was researching a PhD because a scholarship had permitted me to defer any actual choice about what I was going to do and where I was going to do it. I wanted to do everything *except* become an academic. Write books. Play music. Read everything. Travel everywhere. But I was afraid of my own passion, and corralled it by accepting the scholarship and hiding out in the University of Sydney library. Serious budding academics were devoting themselves to literary theory and years of research to the exclusion of other interests; they weren't hanging out for the weekly opportunity to play jazz with like-minded enthusiasts. And although playing with other musicians was thrilling, I knew the workshops weren't the path to professional musicianship: serious jazz musicians were auditioning for the Jazz Studies course at the Conservatorium of Music. At this stage, a sense of purpose, a goal for my research, a vision for my life—or a boyfriend—might have helped.

Jeff, a sweet-natured bank teller, literally and musically speaking stood head and shoulders above the other amateur singers. A veteran of Freddy Wilson's workshops, Jeff lived to sing jazz standards. Endlessly cheerful, he stood well over six feet tall and sported a mop of thick blond hair and a soft clear voice. He'd walk up Freddy's unlit driveway at night, scat-singing as a warm-up exercise before class. Whenever I heard the line 'Why not take all of me?' floating out of the pitch-dark, I knew instantly it was Jeff and felt bad that my immediate next thought was *No thanks*.

One night towards the end of my first term, Jeff handed me a cassette tape. 'It's my demo,' he said. 'Have a listen and let me know what you think.'

Looking down, I saw that he had photocopied a black and white photograph of himself smiling directly at the camera and used it to line the cassette's plastic casing. I pictured him in his lunch hour, a home-made tuna sandwich in one hand, lurking near the bank's photocopier.

'I thought maybe you'd like to rehearse with me sometime,' he continued. 'You know, get some gigs as a duo.' Though flattered, for two mutually exclusive reasons I failed to picture myself performing in a suburban restaurant or shopping mall. The first: I was convinced I wasn't remotely good enough to perform in a mall. Second, I had fancied myself playing my own compositions to a packed house at the Village Vanguard rather than jazz favourites at Chatswood Chase. But without making a choice, my fantasies of a creative professional life would remain just that.

♫

Despite my reservations, a few weeks later I headed to Jeff's apartment. It seemed appropriate that he lived in a suburb called Neutral Bay. Historically, Neutral Bay was one harbour in which foreign vessels could safely dock, and I felt few qualms about rehearsing there with Jeff. He welcomed me with a cup of peppermint tea and smiled constantly to put me at ease, which had precisely the opposite effect. I was no Madame Bovary. Instead of inventing piano lessons in order to meet my lover, I had abandoned years of classical piano lessons and chosen instead to rehearse jazz standards with a bank teller to whom I felt no flicker of attraction.

We warmed up for a few minutes before Jeff said, apropos of nothing, 'Freddy thinks you're a shit-hot piano player.'

I took a gulp of hot tea and a moment to digest. It was the first scrap of feedback I'd had about my months-long participation in the workshops, and it wasn't what I'd expected. What did it mean to be 'shit-hot'? The phrase sounded oxymoronic—not to mention moronic. Was this how real musicians spoke about each other? If so, I would have to toughen up my ears to the professional language of jazz musicians if I wanted to be taken seriously. Clearly I was spending too much time among the dead poets on the library shelves.

But I could neither truly picture myself as a professional musician—the late-night gigs and the lack of money, supplementing performance opportunities with wedding gigs and teaching—nor feel comfortable with the label *amateur*. The outside chance of playing professionally cast a shameful light on just playing for fun. Perhaps it was my father's voice in my ear as a teenager, the self-made man urging my brother and me to make ourselves financially self-sufficient by the age of forty (however one was supposed to do that); or perhaps it was my mother's voice, repeatedly insisting that I always have my own money separate from a man's. Either way I was fixated on the necessity of having a 'proper job' even as I avoided the workforce with the postgraduate scholarship and scraped by living under my parents' roof.

In a *Peanuts* cartoon strip, Lucy van Pelt asks Schroeder: 'What happens if you practise for twenty years, and then end up not being rich and famous?'

'The joy is in the playing,' he says.

'You're kidding!' says Lucy.[57]

Why couldn't I learn Schroeder's lesson? I would have discontinued my PhD and forged ahead with the jazz workshops, instead of the other way around. But Jeff and I never tried very hard to get a gig, and I stopped attending the workshops. Unlike Schroeder, I felt ashamed of my amateurism. Somehow I couldn't simply enjoy being a competent pianist for its own sake. Playing solely for fun seemed pointless—especially when I had few job prospects and a dissertation to write.

31

After the incident with the baritone, Alice stopped singing in public. 'Mrs Lloyd let Mr Palmer put his arm around her!' went the refrain around Yeoval district, my aunt Charlotte recalled, when the pair performed the duet 'I'll Walk with You' at the annual end of year concert in a manner that the locals judged overly enthusiastic. It was the hair-trigger the Baptists had been waiting for ever since Alice Lloyd had arrived in their town with her thick Scottish accent, her astonishing soprano voice, and her lack of humour.

Alice must have wondered how it was possible to travel halfway around the world only to end up in the same place as she'd started. *Da capo.* She might as well have been back in Mrs Rankin's haberdashery among the inane chatter of dagger-mouthed women. She abandoned performance for accompanying. At the piano she could see everything yet remain invisible.

'I don't recall Mum singing at home,' Charlotte said when we talked about her childhood. 'She never sang with me. She wasn't very interested in girls. I had a hearing impediment that wasn't diagnosed until I was fourteen. But I do remember her spending a lot of time with Jimmy, trying to get him to sit up.'

James Lloyd, born in 1925, made few sounds and couldn't sit up by himself. At what point does a parent suspect something is not quite as it should be with their child? There are too many unanswerable questions here. Did Alice know there was a problem and George refuse to acknowledge it, or was it the other way around? As James grew from chubby baby to toddler, they must have sought doctors' opinions for their little boy, who remained floppy as a ragdoll. Whether it was through a local doctor or Nance, George and Alice learned of the Stockton Mental Hospital, on a peninsula across the Hunter River from Newcastle. Opened in 1917, Stockton catered to adults and children with intellectual disabilities. From the very little public information available about this facility, it appears that patients of all ages were housed together. Not until 1937 was there a call for tenders to build a dedicated children's wing.[58]

I'm trying to imagine the agonising journey to Newcastle, George staring straight ahead, his lips tightly drawn, his bony hands gripping the wheel of their green kerosene-powered truck. They left Charlotte, now three, with Nance and Richard. Alice, clutching a sleeping Jimmy to her chest, was most likely relieved that Charlotte wouldn't witness them leaving her brother in the care of strangers.

From what Charlotte remembers, Alice regarded her daughter with a detachment she could not shake. I wonder if she felt Charlotte belonged to George in some way that she did not belong to her, and whether she thought it was due to their relentlessly positive outlook on life.

There would have been a chain of correspondence with Stockton, containing no end of assurances about the quality of care they provided, the expertise, the years of experience helping other children with the same condition as Jimmy. 'We've done all we can for him at home, love,' I can hear George saying. 'They'll know how to help him.' How could Alice argue with the truth?

Even so, the most practical of mothers would feel anguish handing the care of her child to an institution full of strangers—all well-meaning, but none of them his mother. Was Alice tearful or tight-lipped? Weeping or stoic? Did she suffer catastrophic visions of Jimmy alone, cold, crying out for the comfort only a mother provides a toddler? Had she lain awake at night as the date approached, seeing flashes of Jimmy screaming for help, sick with the feeling that she shouldn't be leaving him no matter how qualified the Stockton people presented themselves to be? I am convinced that even after so many years, Alice would still have found it impossible to trust anyone. But there was no logical reason why Jimmy would be better off staying on the farm. And so George and Alice Lloyd committed their little boy into the care of the Stockton Mental Hospital.

Less than one year later, Jimmy contracted dysentery and died there, under the supervision of those who had been charged with his care. He was two and a half.

♫

'When Jimmy died they were stripping the wheat,' my aunt Charlotte recalled, close to ninety years after her brother's death. 'And the wheat could not wait for grief.'

The wheat, the seasons, the dawn and the sunset—life ruthlessly continues, and to those struggling with loss of one kind or another it can feel pretty isolating, if not downright insulting, for time to keep ticking over while your world has collapsed.

I can imagine that stripping the wheat, or any of the seasonal activities of a farming life, might have provided ritual comfort to Alice, even if she felt as empty as the cloudless Yeoval sky. But she wasn't close to her daughter, and she and George must have nearly broken from having to bury their son.

Did she fantasise about returning to Glasgow, or dream of making another fresh start? I doubt it. Alice Lloyd was nothing if not practical. She would have rolled up her sleeves and got on with whatever jobs needed doing, even if she felt dead inside.

32

A YEAR AND A HALF AFTER my husband died, I moved to New York. I was thirty-six. I wanted a break with everything that was familiar to me, in a place that had always been my beacon. I had a green card, and I knew three people who lived there: a married couple, and an ex-boyfriend. It was a start.

But four years later, I had reluctantly started to think about returning to live in Australia. Though it's a big place, New York is also a small town, and freelance writer-editors without a strong network of contacts are as common as muck. Skype had become my professional lifeline because most of my work came from Australia. I had enough—just—but it felt tenuous. Outside work, I went on dates generated by algorithms that, in person, had no rhythm of their own. Inevitably I would have to tell my story and, for most suitors, *widow* was a curiosity killer. I had no piano in my apartment, but I carried my metaphorical piano stool like Schroeder did his toy piano. It didn't seem to matter where I was; I kept men at a manageable distance. Which is to say that I kept myself at a safe distance from everyone else.

Widowed for more than five years, I still hadn't moved on with my life. Perhaps it looked from the outside that I had—after all, I had given up a salaried corporate job for the freelance life; I had sold or given away most of my possessions and rented out my house; I had moved country. For a while I even had what Stevie Wonder called a *part-time lover.* But inside, I didn't feel that much had changed. Most of the actions I'd taken since my husband died were about renunciation—giving up things, just as I had done in abandoning the piano after I failed at the Chopin competition. I hadn't replaced what I'd farewelled with a hopeful vision of my future and a clear plan to achieve it. I felt as though I were treading water. The water just happened to be in the northern hemisphere. I had longed to be free and to be anonymous in the big city: I was both, and I was lonely. What I really wanted, I realised, was to experience love and intimacy again. I was, after all, human. That goal felt small, and immense, and impossible.

I lived in the tiniest bedroom of a decrepit three-bedroom apartment on St John's Place in the Prospect Heights neighbourhood of Brooklyn, which hugs the north-eastern tip of Prospect Park. It is—or was—the poor cousin to the more prosperous Park Slope, the location for many independent films about angst-ridden thirty-somethings. My flatmate Derek worked at a nearby cafe, Cheryl's Global Soul on Underhill Street, while he tried to further his career as a cartoonist and illustrator. Due to the dimensions of my room, which I referred to as *the cabin*, I did my writing and editing at Cheryl's, or at the Brooklyn Public Library on Eastern Parkway, two blocks from our doorstep. We picked up our essentials from the corner store, which we dubbed the *cat-piss bodega* due to its persistent odour. A pair of running shoes was slung over the telegraph lines at our nearest intersection, just like you see in the movies. The neighbourhood was quiet, except for the very occasional gunshot.

Derek was an excellent cook, and he and I would feed each other if we happened to be home together. One morning he announced that he had invited around a friend to share dinner with us that evening. I smiled when he told me, but I had been dreading it all day—the last time a friend of his had joined us for a meal, I had retreated to my cabin after an excruciating attempt at conversation.

This time the friend was a fellow cartoonist, from the Midwest, who had only recently moved to New York. When people ask me how Nate and I met, I like to say that he walked into my kitchen. He was handsome, funny, intelligent, and refreshingly unperturbed by the fact that I was a widow. To top it all off, he loved jazz. Our first date was at a now-defunct jazz bar called Puppets in Park Slope, where the tenor saxophone of Noah Preminger was so loud we had to shout at each other. Which is the only time in the eight years since that we've done that.

33

In April 1934, six years after Jimmy's death, George and Alice again made the journey to Newcastle in the old green kerosene-powered truck, this time with ten-year-old Charlotte squeezed between them. At Newcastle Hospital they signed the final papers and collected a healthy three-month-old boy with wisps of white-blond hair. Who knows why his mother had been forced to abandon him. Well, I'm sure that Alice suspected why, and that she was relieved she hadn't ended up pregnant with John Henry Edwards' child. I wonder if the relief of not having to face an unwanted pregnancy, and a likely forced adoption, had softened the pain of his lies and her humiliation. Pregnancy by a bigamist would not have been a good look in Partick parish in 1918—and especially not for the choirmistress.

But now, Alice and George officially had a new son: John. Did it bother Alice that her son shared the name of the bigamist? Perhaps, being such a common name, it was easier to bear as sheer coincidence. According to my aunt Charlotte, John was the name that his biological mother had chosen for him, and that was good enough for Alice. Staring at her new baby, I can only imagine how Alice's heart burst with love for him as she yearned for James, the son she had lost. I wonder if she thought much over the years about the woman who gave my father up for adoption—and about whether the agony of giving up a baby and wondering, year in, year out, where he was, how he was, who he was, and dying without ever seeing him again, would be even more difficult than burying one's own child.

Under any circumstances, the decision to adopt a child is enormous. But for Alice and George Lloyd, having raised a daughter for ten years and having endured the loss of a son, to take on the care of a newborn baby was an act of almost

unfathomable hope. Their generosity in adopting John does not quite gel in my mind with the apparent lack of maternal feeling Alice displayed toward Charlotte, or her severity to other members of her family. Such as her daughter-in-law, my mother.

'Your father was Mummy's little soldier,' Aunt Charlotte told me. 'She always preferred boys.'

John, who grew up knowing he was adopted, never felt compelled to find his birth mother. Over the years, whenever I asked him about it, he said, 'I had a happy childhood, and I knew I was loved.' John survived the inherent life-limiting risks of a bush upbringing, endured every minute of school until he could leave at fifteen, and worked in his father's stock and station agency. Too young to go to war, John moved to Sydney to live with Charlotte, who had married and moved there five years earlier. In 1955, when he met my mother Pamela at Vic's Cabaret at Strathfield, in Sydney's inner west, John was twenty-one, and a busy subcontractor to builders and property developers.

'He was the nicest man I'd ever met,' my mother told me.

34

It's a warm summer evening on the corner of West End Avenue and 86th Street, and I'm sitting in a cavernous church. But I'm not in a pew, and I'm not taking Communion. I'm seated at a beat-up old grand piano, as a member of an amateur jazz ensemble. Twenty years after Freddy Wilson's workshop, I've progressed from a converted garage to another repurposed structure. And it's a broad church, too: all around me in the warrens of the building are acting classes, exercise classes, and self-defence and martial arts classes. But the jazz ensemble gets to play the main stage.

To my right sits Corporate Mike with his honey-coloured acoustic guitar, which he must have brought directly from his office downtown. On the other side of him is Marcellus from Washington Heights forty blocks north, who waits tables at Dizzy's in Columbus Circle when he's not playing his tenor. In front of me is the gently spoken Pablo on bass; and a pimply monosyllable is at the drum kit who, depending on the night, could be Joe, Sam, Scott or Dave. The drummers look like children, because they are, while the rest of us have a few more runs on the board. Sometimes we're joined by a singer who crosses the Hudson from New Jersey to get here, and sometimes by an older guitarist who, when not practising his instrument, is a practising cardiologist. For a while during the summer we even had an elderly tuba player from Switzerland. A jazz ensemble is one of the few places on Earth where you will reliably find people from different generations listening to each other with attention, respect and genuine interest.

Tonight, like we do every week, we warm up with a blues tune. This time it's Thelonious Monk's 'Blue Monk'. Playing a blues is the conditioning stretch for a jazz band, because it has a common twelve-bar structure that allows us to play ourselves into readiness for the more complicated chord progressions in the three or four other pieces we'll play during the two-hour workshop. Within the twelve-bar harmonic progression of a blues song, almost infinite variation is possible, which is mind-blowing if you consider that the most basic blues progression uses just three chords—the first, the fourth and fifth—of any chosen key. So for a blues in A, for example, your chord progression uses A, D and E. That's it. Its simplicity also explains why so many popular songs across all genres are, at their core, blues progressions (conjure up the *Batman* television theme song), and why—if you're a pop guitarist, a jazz pianist or a budding singer of any stripe—learning the blues is one of the best things you can do to develop your skills. If you are so inclined, you have a lifetime of homework to do—listening to great recordings, practising chord voicings, learning to transpose into different keys, transcribing and imitating great solos—but for the beginner and the advanced student alike, it all comes back to knowing your scales in every key.

In the *Well-Tempered Clavier*, Johann Sebastian Bach composed a prelude and fugue for the keyboard in every one of the twenty-four major and minor keys. His purpose, stated on the dedication of the original 1722 publication, was 'for the profit and use of musical youth desirous of learning, and especially for the pastime of those already skilled in this study'. In terms of the time I have to devote to the piano, and the level of dexterity I enjoy these days, I'm a long way from my early encounters with Bach's foundational work, when I was one of those 'musical youth desirous of learning'. But now in my forties, reflecting on the composer's dedication, I'm struck by his second target audience: 'for the pastime of those already skilled in this study'. He's right—learning is a pastime, an endeavour worth doing for its own sake. As a formal student, whether at school or university or in piano lessons, I always associated learning with a goal or end point that lay beyond the here and now: good grades, graduation, the performance diploma. As an adult returning to the piano after a long and self-enforced separation, I'm taking up Bach's challenge in the environment of the jazz workshop. I'm not sure what Johann Sebastian would think about my choice, but I've decided that I'll be doing pretty well if I can learn to improvise over a blues progression in any of those twenty-four keys. There's no greater goal to that pastime than improving how I play with other amateur musicians. And what a relief that is.

Once each instrumentalist has taken a chorus of 'Blue Monk', our teacher Ron, a professional trumpet player and arranger, asks the group which song we'd like to play first. We choose from a shortlist nominated by the students at the end of last week's workshop. Our weekly homework is to familiarise ourselves with the chord charts for each piece, to learn the melody accurately and to study the basic structure, so that next week we can simply start playing it together.

'When you go all over the world and you know a handful of tunes, you can speak to each other,' Ron says, as if each of us were planning to sit in at a jazz club jam session the next time we're visiting Paris. And just like Freddy, Ron is full of aphorisms:

'There's the notes versus the spirit of a piece.'

'We have to play with confidence.'

'Play it wrong but play it strong.'

'Great solos have an arc, a shape to them.'

'When we play we want to get out of our heads entirely.'

I'd say that last one is my favourite, though it remains aspirational. I still find myself counting bars as the other band members play their solos, trying to make sure I don't lose my place. The pianist needs to give the soloist the occasional harmonic or melodic reminder as to where in the chorus he is—at the end of the second A-section moving into the bridge (or B-section); coming toward the end of the bridge and going back to A, for example—so it's pretty important I know where I am. Inevitably each of us gets lost at some point during a workshop, but the beauty of the group is that usually we're not all lost in the same tune at the same time, and so one of us can lead the others out of the musical wilderness.

In my early years of living in New York, I spent a lot of time attending jazz gigs by myself. At the Village Vanguard, the 55 Bar and Smalls, mainly, a short stroll from each other along Seventh Avenue South in Greenwich Village.

Sometimes I'd have company, but the lack of it never stopped me attending a gig by a musician I really wanted to hear play.

One of the greatest aspects of the live jazz scene in New York is the sense of being among a community of kindred spirits. As a woman, I found the clubs to be an incredibly liberating environment. You can sit at the bar or stand at the back nursing your drink, and enjoy the music without having to keep your peripheral vision alert for the approach of unsolicited company. You can chat with the bartender if you want to, but there's no obligation to socialise. As a woman by yourself, you will be left alone unless you initiate conversation. And those times when I did smile back at a friendly stranger or initiate a conversation, I usually found the interactions to be worth having.

After more than two decades of listening to live jazz performances, my enjoyment has not dimmed. I love watching the musicians respond to each other, fearlessly open in the moment of performance; unselfconscious so that they can react spontaneously, creating improvised lines of melody and accompaniment that are instantaneous but informed by years of listening, knowledge and practice under the heat of spotlights without a safety net. It's fun, it's inspiring, and at times it feels almost sacred. A transporting live jazz performance feeds that part of me not nourished by reading or friendship or travel or sex. The playful part that needs connection to others through music-making. And the desire to feel that connection is what, finally, drove me to seek out the opportunity to play again with others.

The fact that I'm the only woman instrumentalist in the jazz ensemble sometimes bothers me. It was the same in Freddy Wilson's workshops, all those years ago. The only thing that has changed in the interim is that we now use an app to access music charts. Is this passion of mine really so gendered? Are there so few other women interested in playing jazz with others? I guess that other women my age have less flexible schedules—careers that demand long hours at the office, and children who demand long hours everywhere else. And perhaps young musical women are more interested in being singer-songwriters or are too busy either finishing a degree or paying off student debt. It's a shame, though, because despite the ratio of men to women, I find the jazz workshop one of the most gender-neutral group settings I've ever experienced. In the moment of playing, each musician is equally engaged in the act of creation; their gender makes no difference.

In the workshops, nobody has a last name. Nobody has a past. Nobody wants to know what I do before or after the workshop, how I earn a living, or where I live. There's no judgement, just constructive feedback on how to improve my ensemble playing and my solos; no goal greater than self-expression. There are no deadlines, no scaffolding of centuries of pedagogy, no examiners to assess my version of a work against generations of interpretations. It's quite the opposite: the workshop actively encourages me to be myself at the piano, trying to express how I hear the world, within the harmonic, melodic and rhythmic constraints of an ensemble of players who accept them. This interplay of individual expression and group dynamics is why I've always regarded a jazz ensemble as the best expression of democracy in action: freedom of individual expression, facilitated and supported by a framework of musical conventions agreed by consensus.

And now, with Ron's eyebrow raised at me to make sure I know it's my turn, I take my solo. Use an element of the melody, use a rhythmic motif of the preceding soloist, use a musical idea that comes into my head in the moment. Double it, halve it, vary it higher and lower—experiment, fail, try again, fail better. Leave some space. Don't fill every bar with notes; it's okay not to play.

The experience of playing a 32-bar solo with a band is thrilling—playing with the knowledge that there is no meaning in it other than this dense and visceral moment in which time does its peculiar thing of expanding even as it goes by incredibly fast. A microcosm of life, really. There will be no final exam. There will be no recording for posterity—thank goodness. Just performance in the moment. To play like this is to embrace meaninglessness, in its best possible sense.

♫

In 1895, in the last months of her long life, Clara Schumann's daughters insisted she write down some of the preludes she improvised daily before she practised her scales. She did so, but described the difficult work of notating them: '[I]t is so hard because I do it differently each time, as it occurs to me as I sit at the piano.'[59] She had abandoned formal composition at twenty, but improvised new music every day for decades. The demands of the former made her doubt herself; the confidence and liberation of the latter meant that she felt no need for the constraints of writing down the music she made up. How difficult it is for some of us to value a skill that comes easily, whether it's creating music or teaching a child.

For most of my adult life, I had castigated myself for abandoning thirteen years of piano studies and the love of accompanying other musicians for an adult life conducted without much direct contact with a piano. I chose a professional life in book publishing and limited my participation in music to passive consumption: attending live performances and listening to recordings. Like thousands of other musical girls, adulthood had taken me a long way from the piano stool.

My twentieth high school reunion had made me confront that choice and wonder about what I'd lost as a result of making it. At first I despaired at the roads not taken, the lives not lived. I jumped to the demoralising conclusion that all those years of practice, competition and exams had been for nothing. I castigated myself for not using the same time to study a foreign language or HTML, even if the latter had been possible in the 1980s.

As it had been for my grandmother Alice May Morrison Taylor Lloyd, intensive music study and performance had been a crucial part of forming my identity. And, like my grandmother, in response to a crisis I chose to renounce my musicianship. Her decision to leave her burgeoning professional life in Scotland as a choirmistress and well-regarded soprano was much more significant than my decision to abandon the piano and any glimmer of a life in music, but in each case the choice involved a shutting down, rather than an opening up, of possibility.

In her strange new life in New South Wales, Alice taught local students and was the Yeoval Baptist Church accompanist, but her performing opportunities were limited in number and quality. It must have been supremely frustrating to live with the contrast between the musical life she led in her adopted country and the variety and esteem of the one she had left behind. Perhaps the discrepancy gnawed at her unconsciously, because she didn't teach my aunt Charlotte or my father John to play. One must form a fairly negative impression of the value of a musical education to possess that knowledge and not pass it on to your children.

In my own case, I had become so focused on solo performance for the sake of competition and advanced grades, I had forgotten how much I enjoyed playing with others. It was fun, it was pointless, so I stopped. I had renounced any participation in making music and spent years grieving the loss of it, when I'd had no reason to do so other than a misplaced sense of shame at no longer being able to play with the same dexterity or focus I had as an adolescent. My metabolism isn't as fast as it used to be either, but I still eat.

Participating in the jazz ensemble is a humbling lesson every week in the importance of fun. For me it's the perfect meeting point of learning and enjoyment—the same state of joyful self-improvement I had intuited as a child about Schroeder's devotion to the piano in *Peanuts*. I attend each workshop with the refreshing confidence that there is no shame in being an amateur musician. But embracing my amateurism took me a very long time.

Whether we're falling in love, playing the piano, or trying to be a good parent or friend, we are all amateurs. Through study and practice we can acquire expertise or discover a special talent. In most acts of living, though, we're all doing it for the first time, improvising as we go. We connect, we lose, we try again. We're all making choices in limited time within the parameters of our educations, childhoods, the opportunities we've had or lacked. We're all learning to balance the melody and the harmony. To survive, we have to learn how to play solo, and how to play with others.

Each week's workshop is also a sober reminder of my responsibility in the decision to abandon my musicianship: that it was I who had been so afraid of failing, who had used my perfectionism as an excuse to isolate myself, who had cost myself years of enjoyment by closing myself off to the sheer fun of playing music with others. I had learned early in life that isolation was a safe place to be. Later, as a widow, I had done the same thing, closing myself off for many years to the possibility of a new relationship. Now, in our Brooklyn apartment, as I practise on the electronic keyboard that Nate bought me for Christmas, I see they are variations on the same theme.

I believe that my grandmother made a similar choice in coming to Australia and renouncing her musical life in Glasgow: a choice to withdraw rather than embrace, to isolate rather than connect. Even though she established a new life for herself, marrying George and having children, she stopped performing and taught other people's children for money rather than her own for pleasure. I remember how scared I was of her, how little I knew of what she'd loved, lost and left behind. When I think about Alice May Morrison Taylor now, I think of her lovely soprano voice, and how I never heard her sing.

♫

The writer and literary critic Terry Eagleton recently proposed that the very meaning of life is like the workings of a jazz band.

> A jazz group which is improvising obviously differs from a symphony orchestra, since to a large extent

each member is free to express herself as she likes. But she does so with a receptive sensitivity to the self-expressive performances of the other musicians . . . There is no conflict here between freedom and the 'good of the whole', yet the image is the reverse of totalitarian. Though each performer contributes to 'the greater good of the whole', she does so not by some grim-lipped self-sacrifice but simply by expressing herself. There is self-realisation, but only through a loss of self in the music as a whole. There is achievement, but it is not a question of self-aggrandising success. Instead, the achievement—the music itself—acts as a medium of relationship among the performers. There is pleasure to be reaped from this artistry, and—since there is a free fulfilment or realisation of powers—there is also happiness in the sense of flourishing. Because this flourishing is reciprocal, we can even speak, remotely and analogically, of a kind of love. One could do worse, surely, than propose such a situation as the meaning of life—both in the sense that it is what makes life meaningful, and—more controversially—in

> the sense that when we act in this way, we realise our natures at their finest.[60]

Is it crazy to aspire to live like a jazz musician? There are worse things than playing solo and playing with others; expressing myself honestly rather than hiding from vulnerability; aspiring to exist in reciprocity, love, respect and acceptance.

♫

There's an improvised coda to my life's work that no one, not even I, saw coming: my daughter Hazel, who arrived when I was well into my forties. Many women understandably rail against the medical term for a woman who becomes pregnant for the first time after she turns thirty-five, but I could not be happier to have been an *elderly primigravida.*

Hazel sits on my lap and bangs her tiny palms on the black notes and presses her right index finger on the tip of the white ones. Sometimes she likes to play the notes highest up the keyboard, or simply turn the pages of whatever music manuscript is propped open on the stand in front of her.

She's partial now to selections from the *Peanuts Illustrated Songbook*, especially the unmistakable 'Lucy and Linus' that so enchanted my ears as a child. At eighteen months, the printed music fascinates her; most likely due to the high-contrast black marks on white pages. Hazel is getting to know the same piano I started learning on when I was seven, in a house in Sydney not far from the one I grew up in. This apple, via the Big Apple, has landed not far from the tree.

I have concluded that the authorship of one's life is a form of improvisation in which each of us is engaged, like members of an infinite jazz band. While jazz isn't exactly the meaning of life, the dynamics within a jazz ensemble provide a model of community to which, with Eagleton, I believe human society should aspire. Eagleton suggests the goal would be 'to construct this kind of community on a wider scale', while acknowledging the political challenge in achieving it. Utopian, yes, but I'd still vote for that.

Perhaps other girls at the piano didn't regret giving up their lessons or no longer playing with other musicians. Perhaps they did, and got over it. Or in the frenetic jumble of long hours, high-pressure jobs, deadlines, school drop-offs and ballet pick-ups, they folded up and packed away that passionate amateur—the girl obsessed with drawing, or photography, writing, dancing, singing—who was never seen again. In my case she didn't go away, nor did the desire to play music with others, no matter how much I sublimated that desire in attending live jazz and listening to recordings. The physical act of playing the piano was too important to my identity, too central to my first experiences of joy, envy, love, pain, exhilaration and despair.

'The piano was my first mirror and my first awareness of my own face was through blackness, through its translation into blackness, as into a language dark but comprehensible,' Marina Tsvetaeva wrote in 'Mother and Music'. 'That is how it was my whole life: to understand the simplest thing I had to plunge it into poetry, to see it from there.'

Writing about my relationship to the piano has shown me how much I need music and writing in my life. I had always considered them to be intense competitors struggling against each other in a zero-sum game for my attention; they are in fact opposites that depend on each other in the same way that the strength of a bridge is reinforced by equal tension from both sides. Learning the piano intensively for such a long time shaped my way of seeing and hearing the world, reflecting me back to myself. My 'pianohood' of self-discipline, attention to detail, careful listening, exponential learning, competition, failure and the discovery of improvisation affected so many choices I made later in life. It turns out that I have, in fact, *been doing something with the piano* all my life—living with the sensibility and preferences shaped by the experience of passionate attachment to the instrument. These effects of early music training are largely invisible but unmistakable, the ripples in the pond. It's a long way from how my old schoolfriends had expected me to apply my musicianship. If I ran into a former classmate today, I would confidently tell her that yes, I still play the piano. That I love to play it, I need to play it, and at last I understand why. I may never again play with the skill or frequency that I did as a teenager, but I will always think of myself as a pianist.

ENDNOTES

1 Roy E. Wates, *Mozart: An Introduction to the Music, the Man, and the Myths* (Amadeus, 2010): 26.

2 James Parakilas, *Piano Roles: Three Hundred Years of Life with the Piano* (Yale University Press, 2002): 65.

3 Wates, *Mozart*: 26.

4 Feb 25–26, 1778, in Wates, *Mozart*: 27

5 Quoted in Arthur Loesser, *Men, Women and Pianos: A Social History* (Dover Publications, 1990): 102–103.

6 Loesser, *Men, Women and Pianos*: 133.

7 Loesser: viii.

8 Statistics and *Girls Own Annual* taken from Cyril Ehrlich, *The Piano: A History* (Dent, 1976; revised edition Clarendon Press, 1990).

9 Hugh Reginald Haweis, *Music and Morals* (Strahan, 1871): 515.

10 Ehrlich, *The Piano*: 92.

11 Roland Barthes, 'Musica Practica', in *Image Music Text*, essays selected and translated by Stephen Heath (Fontana Press, 1977): 149–154.

12 Ehrlich, *The Piano*: 102.

13 Claire Tomalin, *Jane Austen: A Life* (Knopf, 1998): 211.

14 Robert K. Wallace, *Jane Austen and Mozart: Classical Equilibrium in Fiction and Music* (University of Georgia Press, 1983): 250.

15 Charles Czerny, *Letters to a Young Lady, on the Art of Playing the Pianoforte, from the earliest rudiments to the highest state of cultivation: written as an appendix to every school for that instrument*, trans. J.A. Hamilton (Firth, Pond & Co., 1851): Preface.

16 James Leggio, *Music and Modern Art* (Routledge, 2002): 58 n. 31.

17 David Michaelis, *Schulz and Peanuts: A Biography* (HarperCollins, 2008): 339. It beat out Victor Lasky, *JFK: The Man and the Myth*, in the wake of the president's assassination.

18 Charles M. Schulz, *Play It Again, Schroeder!* (Ballantine, 2007).

19 Maxim Gorky, quoted in Georg Lukacs' 1967 Postscript to his own work, *Lenin: A Study on the Unity of His Thought* (1924).

20 Umberto Eco, 'On "Krazy Kat" and "Peanuts"', translated by William Weaver in the *New York Review of Books*, 13 June 1985.

21 Alexander Wheelock Thayer, *Life of Beethoven*, volume I, edited by Elliot Forbes (Princeton University Press, 1967): 323.

22 Michaelis, *Schulz and Peanuts*: 348.

23 The words are scribbled across a sketch of composed music from c. 1809, reproduced in Lewis Lockwood, *Beethoven: The Music and the Life* (Norton, 2005): 281.

24 Glasgow *Herald*, 25 November 1891.

25 Loesser, *Men, Women and Pianos*: pp. 418–29.

26 All references are to Maria Tsvetaeva, 'Mother and Music', pp. 271–294 in Marina Tsvetaeva, *A Captive Spirit: Selected Prose*, edited and translated by J. Marin King (Ardis, 1980).

27 Yo Tomita, in his essay 'The Inventions and Sinfonias', published online at http://www.music.qub.ac.uk/~tomita/essay/inventions.html and used as the liner notes for Masaaki Suzuki's 1998 recording of the *Inventions*, quotes this translation from the autograph fair copy in the Staatsbibliothek zu Berlin but does not identify the translator from the original German.

28 Letter dated 19 Jan 1864, in *George Eliot's Letters, edited by G.S. Height* (Yale University Press, 1954).

29 Czerny, *Letters to a Young Lady*: 26.

30 François Noudelmann, *The Philosopher's Touch: Sartre, Nietzsche, and Barthes at the Piano*, trans. Brian J. Reilly (Columbia University Press, 2012).

31 Nancy B. Reich, *Clara Schumann: The Artist and the Woman* (Cornell University Press, 1985): 285.

32 Henry Handel Richardson, *Myself When Young* (W.W. Norton & Company, 1948): 117.

33 Henry Handel Richardson: 117.

34 D.H. Lawrence, 'Nottingham and the Mining Countryside', in *Phoenix: The Posthumous Papers of D. H. Lawrence* (Heinemann, 1936), pp. 133–40: 138.

35 There is a Google Group devoted to the attribution of this description.

36 George Holbert Tucker, *Jane Austen the Woman: Some Biographical Insights* (Palgrave Macmillan, 1995): 104.

37 Aaron Williamon, 'Memorising Music', pp. 113–26, in *Musical performance: a guide to understanding, edited by John Rink* (Cambridge University Press, 2002): 113.

38 Reich, *Clara Schumann*: 272.

39 Fred M. Hall, *It's About Time: The Dave Brubeck Story* (University of Arkansas Press, 1996): 63.

40 *In the Course of Performance: Studies in the World of Musical Improvisation*, edited by Bruno Nettle with Melinda Russell (Chicago University Press, 1998): 240.

41 Reich, *Clara Schumann*: 236 n. 66.

42 Czerny, *Letters to a Young Lady*: 74.

43 Nettle, *In the Course of Performance*: 255.

44 Letters dated 10 June and 22 June 1853, in Berthold Litzmann, *Clara Schumann: An Artist's Life Based on Material Found in Diaries and Letters*, volume II (Litzmann Press, 2013): n.p.

45 Loesser, *Men, Women and Pianos*: 422.

46 See William Weber, *The Great Transformation of Musical Taste: Concert Programming from Haydn to Brahms* (Cambridge, 2008).

47 George Eliot, *George Eliot's Life, as Related in Her Letters and Journals*, edited by John Cross (1885; Cambridge University Press, 2010): 26.

48 Williamon, 'Memorising Music': 114.

49 Charles Darwin, *The Descent of Man, and Selection in Relation to Sex* (Appleton, 1871): 272.

50 Charles Darwin: 272.

51 Loesser, *Men, Women and Pianos*: 335.

52 Parakilis, *Piano Roles*: pp. 127–28.

53 Ehrlich, *The Piano*: 97.

54 Wikipedia: https://en.wikipedia.org/wiki/HMAS_Berrima.

55 Holly Brubach, 'A Pianist for Whom Never Was Never an Option', *The New York Times*, 10 June 2007.

56 E. Altenmüller and H.-C. Jabusch. 'Focal Dystonia in Musicians: Phenomenology, Pathophysiology and Triggering Factors', in *European Journal of Neurology* 2010, 17 (Suppl. 1), pp. 31–36: 33.

57 Schulz, *Play It Again, Schroeder!*: 69.

58 https://www.findandconnect.gov.au/ref/nsw/biogs/NE01696b.htm

59 Reich, *Clara Schumann*: 265, n. 65.

60 Terry Eagleton, *The Meaning of Life: A Very Short Introduction* (Oxford University Press, 2008): pp. 98–100.

ACKNOWLEDGEMENTS

This book originated with my enduring love for the piano, which I thank my parents for cultivating. They encouraged my interest in music and bought me that upright Yamaha, which I now play with and for my daughter.

My aunt Charlotte Butler, now 94, has been a generous source of inspiration, documentation, anecdote and insight into her own childhood and the life of her mother Alice.

During the writing process, Ian Hicks buoyed my sometimes flagging spirits in New York with occasional long-distance calls from Hobart to ask after the book's progress.

I'm very grateful to Geoff Dyer for selecting me to work with him at a residency at the remarkable Atlantic Center for the Arts in 2013—and for the tennis.

Old friends Daniela Fornasaro and Kelsey Bray provided details from adolescence that prodded my own memories or filled in details I had lost, while Derek Van Giesen sustained me at the Oneida with cocktails, meals, music and humour.

Madeleine Beckman, Lily Brett, Madonna Duffy and Jennifer Fleming provided constructive feedback in addition to friendship.

At Allen & Unwin, I was delighted to find a simpatico publisher in Jane Palfreyman. I am particularly indebted to Ali Lavau for an editorial report that helped me see how to get to where I wanted the manuscript to go. And my thanks to Siobhán Cantrill and Kate Goldsworthy for fine-tuning the instrument.

As my friend and mentor, Mary Folliet was unflagging in her support for this project from its earliest stages, and always knew the right questions to ask. Her understanding, encouragement and hospitality were invaluable to the development of this book.

I could not have written this book without the love of Nate Neal, who has been by my side almost as long as this manuscript.

♫

Image of Dumbarton Road, Glasgow, reproduced with kind permission of Glasgow Life.

'Late Autumn' by V. Evstafieff showing Emma Darwin at the piano reproduced by courtesy of Historic England.

Extract from *The Children's Bach* by Helen Garner published by Penguin Books. Reprinted by permission of Penguin Random House Australia Pty Ltd.

Extracts from *Myself When Young* by Henry Handel Richardson by arrangement with the Licensor, The Henry Handel Richardson Estate, c/- Curtis Brown (Aust) Pty Ltd.

A Captive Spirit by Marina Tsvetaeva, translated and edited by J. Marin King. Reprinted by arrangement with The Overlook Press, Peter Mayer Publishers, Inc. www.overlookpress.com/ardis.html.

Extracts from *This Real Night* by Rebecca West reprinted by permission of Peters Fraser & Dunlop (www.petersfraser-dunlop.com) on behalf of the Estate of Rebecca West.